FROM TRUST TO TRAGEDY

FROM TRUST TO TRAGEDY

The Political Memoirs of Frederick Nolting,
Kennedy's Ambassador to Diem's Vietnam

FREDERICK NOLTING

Foreword by
William Colby

New York
Westport, Connecticut
London

Library of Congress Cataloging-in-Publication Data

Nolting, Frederick.
　From trust to tragedy : the political memoirs of Frederick
Nolting, Kennedy's ambassador to Diem's Vietnam / Frederick Nolting
; foreword by William Colby.
　　　p.　cm.
　　Bibliography: p.
　　Includes index.
　　ISBN 0–275–93080–7 (alk. paper).　ISBN 0–275–93106–4 (pbk. : alk.
paper)
　　　1. United States—Foreign relations—Vietnam.　2. Vietnam—Foreign
relations—United States.　3. United States—Foreign
relations—1961–1963.　4. Vietnamese Conflict, 1961–1975—United
States.　5. Nolting, Frederick.　6. Ambassadors—United States—
Biography.　I. Title.
E183.8.V5N66　1988
327.730597—dc19　　　88–15397

Library of Congress Catalog Card Number: 88–15397
ISBN: 0–275–93080–7
ISBN: 0–275–93106–4 (pbk.)

First Published in 1988

Praeger Publishers, One Madison Avenue, New York, NY　10010
A division of Greenwood Press, Inc.

Printed in the United States of America

∞

The paper used in this book complies with the Permanent
Paper Standard issued by the National Information Standards
Organization (Z39.48—1984).

10　9　8　7　6　5　4　3　2　1

To those who tried
and to those who died
for a free Vietnam.

Contents

Illustrations

Foreword

Frederick Nolting was appointed by President Kennedy to serve as his ambassador to South Vietnam at a critical time. He came to Vietnam in 1961 without experience in Asia. He did have long and successful experience in smoothing relationships between a dominant United States and the European nations just beginning to assert themselves after the trauma of World War II. He quickly perceived that the task before him in Vietnam was comparable, if much more difficult. Nationalism among the former colonies of the West in that region was even more intense than in Europe, which had the self-assuredness of centuries of national identity. In Vietnam, the task was magnified by the fact that the two contenders for power there, Ho Chi Minh in the North and Ngo Dinh Diem in the South, both asserted their nationalist credentials. Since Ho had actually defeated the French colonial power, Diem's task was to equal Ho's nationalism even though he fully realized that he depended on American support to rally a shattered South Vietnam and make it a nation.

Shortly before Nolting's arrival in Saigon, Ho and his colleagues decided to relaunch the "people's war" against South Vietnam, which they had so successfully carried out against the French. They denominated their enemy the "American-Diemists" in an effort to characterize the struggle as a continuing one of nationalism against a new American colony. Nolting's task was to support the Southern government and to understand its need to assert its nationalist credentials even against the United States, on whom it depended. He did a superb job. He developed the closest of relations with the leadership of the new nation and influenced it by persuasion as a friend, not pressure by an adversary.

But Nolting had to contend with another constituency—the Kennedy administration that had sent him to Vietnam and its natural sensitivity to American public opinion. This constituency found flaws in the Mandarin regime Diem exemplified as failing to match the democratic standards the United States held up for itself and insisted on for its clients and dependents.

The American press corps in Vietnam focused on the fact that Vietnam was managed in an authoritarian, however benevolent, fashion and that Diem's missionary zeal to modernize his nation met resistance from many who preferred other directions. And when the enemy pressure grew as the North stepped up its efforts, the regime was faulted for its failings in meeting them. The American establishment, especially in Washington, was divided between those who called for a more effective military response to the North and those who asserted that Diem's rule was too undemocratic to rally his nation for defense. The eventual result, against Ambassador Nolting's advice, was American complicity in the overthrow and murder of Diem, and a period of political chaos and confusion in Vietnam that President Lyndon Johnson felt compelled to respond to by the commitment of a massive American expeditionary force.

As this drama unfolded, Nolting retained a clear and persistent view that the United States should support the constituted authority in Vietnam which Diem represented and that it should persevere in the strategy of helping the Diem government to win its own struggle against the Viet Cong, through such programs as the strategic hamlets. He fought for his policies from Saigon to Washington and against some of the towering figures of the Kennedy administration. In the end he lost that battle, but his story of it is a necessary piece of American history. It is made more important because in retrospect it is clear that the policies he fought against proved to be massively mistaken and engulfed America in a war which shook it internally and which it lost. As we face other challenges around the world, and even close to home in Central America, this account by a far-sighted Virginia gentleman of our early Vietnam experience deserves particular attention.

William E. Colby
Director of Central Intelligence, 1973–1976;
currently Counsel with Donovan Leisure Newton & Irvine,
Washington, D.C.

Preface

Twenty-eight years ago, when President Kennedy asked me to serve as his Ambassador to South Vietnam, a friend told me that Vietnam puts a blight on everyone who touches it—a blight of frustration, futility, and failure. I remember taking the remark lightly, but it has come to mind from time to time over the years. The French have a similar belief or superstition. They call it *le mal jaune*, connoting a deep compassion and nostalgia for Indo-China and its people.

Ironies, frustrations, reversals, and failures abound in the records of Americans who have touched Vietnam.

President John F. Kennedy, in framing American relations with South Vietnam early in his administration, pledged to President Ngo Dinh Diem that the United States would increase its aid to South Vietnam. He also pledged not to interfere in the internal political affairs of that country. Two years later, President Kennedy publicly called for "changes in policy and perhaps in personnel" in President Diem's government. "If it doesn't make those changes," he said, "I would think that the chances of winning would not be very good." To reinforce his words, American aid in certain categories was cut off. Revolutionary forces in Vietnam were made bold for the coup. In November 1963, an era that began on a note of mutual confidence and trust ended tragically for both countries, with the assassinations of both presidents.

Lyndon Johnson, when he was Vice President, opposed American measures designed to coerce the Diem government. He had been to Vietnam and correctly sensed the dangers of a military coup d'etat in that unruly and hard-pressed country. Ironically, President Johnson inherited from President Kennedy the consequences of Diem's overthrow and assassination. Unwilling to draw back from the abyss, he vainly attempted to fill Vietnam's political vacuum with American military forces. He ultimately retired from the Presidency overwhelmed by his Vietnam legacy and his failure to resolve it.

Dean Rusk, as Secretary of State, failed, in my view, to supply the oversight required in American policy toward Southeast Asia in the early 1960s, when the problems there were more political than military. True, he was preoccupied with larger issues, in particular the tense confrontations with the Soviet Union over Berlin and Cuba. Yet later, when Vietnam grew into a real war, Rusk became a last-ditch defender of American military involvement.

Robert S. McNamara, as Secretary of Defense, early strove to build South Vietnam's self-reliance and capacity for self-defense without the use of foreign forces. He was the principal member of Kennedy's cabinet to support and encourage our initial policy there. Yet it was McNamara who presided over the buildup and deployment of half a million American combat troops—a development he later deplored.

Mike Mansfield, the Senate's majority leader, was considered by President Diem to be his oldest and most understanding American friend. Yet Senator Mansfield (perhaps unwittingly) drove the first nail into Diem's coffin by his report to President Kenedy in 1962, condemning his old friend. The Mansfield report said in essence that Diem had lost touch with his people and was increasingly isolated from them, a view which my own observations did not sustain.

Senator William Fulbright, then Chairman of the Senate Foreign Relations Committee, was at first a strong supporter of American aid to South Vietnam. He was encouraging to our mission and very helpful in his suggestions at a Senate committee hearing in January 1962. Later, he was sponsor of the sweeping Tonkin Gulf Resolution. But after that, changing his mind, he vigorously opposed further military involvement and, several years too late, tried to shackle the Chief Executive by challenging his power to fight an undeclared war.

Averell Harriman, President Kennedy's special representative during negotiations on Laos in 1961–62, became Assistant Secretary of State for Southeast Asian Affairs in 1962 and later Under Secretary for Political Affairs. He became the top State Department official dealing with Vietnam in the early 1960s. Despite his long and distinguished service to our country in other fields, Harriman's judgment and direction of policy toward Southeast Asia were, in my opinion, disastrous. His attempt to "neutralize" Laos was a dismal failure, and his growing hostility to President Diem and his family became a major factor in Diem's overthrow. Harriman's prestige and political influence in Washington, however, were so great as to become decisive in the crucial actions our government took in 1963.

Henry Cabot Lodge assured me in Honolulu in August 1963 (in conferences on his way to Saigon as Ambassador) that he knew of no intention in Washington to change the long-standing American policy of supporting South Vietnam through its elected constitutional government. Nevertheless, within a week, Ambassador Lodge was officially encouraging a group of Vietnamese generals to overthrow their legitimate government. In a cable to Secretary Rusk (August 29, 1963), Lodge said, "We are launched on a course from which there is no respectable turning back: the overthrow of the Diem government." After the coup produced results quite opposite from those he and others expected, Lodge said in an interview with the *New York Times* (June 30, 1964): "The U.S. was not involved in the overthrow of the Diem regime. . . . The overthrow was a purely Vietnamese affair." In this, he was only echoing the now discredited official line.

The history of American involvement in Vietnam is replete with errors— and I was certainly not immune to them. It also contains shining examples of our nation's capacity for acts of dedication, compassion, fortitude, imagi- nation, and courage. The tragedy is that our political mistakes, outweighing our successes and obscuring our motives, led our country into an unnecessary war, with all its bitter consequences.

In this account (which is not a history but an interpretation) I have tried to cast some light on the events in Vietnam and Washington that culminated in the overthrow of the Diem government in November 1963. If it contributes to an understanding of where we went wrong in Vietnam and for what reasons, perhaps it will also help us in our present and future decisions.

Acknowledgments

Many people deserve my thanks for their contributions toward the completion and publication of these memoirs. First and foremost, my beloved wife and intrepid partner is largely responsible for its completion. I can not come even close to expressing adequately my debt of gratitude to her over the years. Two of our daughters, Lindsay Nolting and Frances Temple, gave generously of their time and talents, as well as their knowledge of people and events in this narrative. And to complete the family circle, I am grateful to our other daughters, Molly Bruner and Jane Meniktos, for their faith, encouragement, and help. All of them served, in one way or another, to promote American objectives in Vietnam.

The late Walker Cowan, former director of the University Press of Virginia, gave me the first "green light" toward publication. I have sorely missed his help and encouragement.

Mildred Vasan at Greenwood Press picked up the manuscript after Walker Cowan's death. She has since given me valuable help and advice, as has David L. Young, Production Editor at Greenwood, and to them, I am greatly indebted.

Among our Vietnamese friends, I am especially grateful to former Minister Nguyen Dinh Thuan of the Republic of Vietnam. Over many years of correspondence and discussion, Thuan's knowledge, insights, and personal friendship have been both a pleasure and an invaluable asset. While he may not agree with all of my views and assessments, I am confident that he agrees with the major thesis of this book, both with regard to his own countrymen and our own.

Here at the University of Virginia, I am indebted to many friends and colleagues on the faculty, in particular to Professor Kenneth Thompson, Director of the White Burkett Miller Center for Public Affairs, and to Professor David Jordan, recently U.S. Ambassador to Peru. Both of these scholars read the manuscript in draft and gave me valuable advice and comments from their extensive knowledge and experience.

My colleague in the Foreign Service and close friend, Murat W. Williams, former Ambassador to El Salvador, read the manuscript and helped me greatly, particularly through his insights into the problems of developing countries and how the United States should—and should not—deal with them.

Suzanne Coffman, historian in the State Department Office of Historical Research, deserves special thanks for her work on this manuscript. On her own time, she read and condensed many pages of oral history which I had recorded over the years at the request of several institutions, adding material omitted from the manuscript and checking many points against official records when they were declassified. She also provided me with much unofficial material and many public documents to refresh my memory. Largely as a result of her help, I am satisfied with the accuracy of this account. I should add that Ms. Coffman's assistance, while authorized by her office, in no way implies the endorsement of the Department of State. The interpretations, selection of materials, and authorship of this work are my own responsibility.

Believing as I do that the tide of history and public judgment about events described herein has shifted greatly over the past decades, I am grateful to all those who have encouraged me to publish my long-held convictions.

FROM TRUST TO TRAGEDY

Introduction

Even in Dalat, a resort area in the Central Highlands, the weather was sultry on this May afternoon in 1961, though far less sultry than in Saigon. The poinsettias, blooming everywhere, were a dark red, noticeably darker than those in the lowlands. Against the green background of pine trees and firs, they made one think of Christmas at home, despite the season and the weather.

Dalat seemed a peaceful town in those days. It had the air of a slightly run-down but still fashionable mountain resort, a pleasant mixture of French colonial architecture and Vietnamese gaiety and color. The President of the Republic, Ngo Dinh Diem, was staying in Dalat for the weekend, and many Vietnamese flags were flying. A few armed guards were stationed unobtrusively in the town against a possible Viet Cong raid.

My wife and I and three of our daughters were quartered in a house known as "Bao Dai's Second Concubine's Villa."[1] It was an extraordinary house, particularly the double bathroom with a mirrored ceiling. Every effort had been made to make us comfortable, and we were. After the steamy heat of Saigon, it was pleasant to see a fireplace in the living room with pine logs ready to burn at night. Mosquito spray was thick in the air, a precaution against the mountain mosquitos that carry malaria.

Just before two o'clock in the afternoon, I set out to call on President Ngo Dinh Diem. We were to have our first private talk about the possibilities and means of closer collaboration between our countries. Diem had asked for this talk in Dalat, where there would be time and a less oppressive atmosphere in which to discuss the many matters flowing from important recent events in Saigon and Washington. I had not yet gotten to know President Diem well. In the two weeks my family and I had been in Vietnam, the time had been crowded with the visit of Vice President Johnson and his party, and, while there had been several serious discussions and a round of social gatherings, the Vietnamese President and I had not had the chance to talk privately at length or to size up one another.

It is often the case that, after concentrated study and briefing, the main elements of a decision remain in doubt until the human element—the evaluation of a person—becomes clear and definite. Sometimes this takes weeks, months, or even years. On the brief drive from the "Concubine's Villa" to President Diem's unpalatial residence, I thought of the many different views held about this man in America. Was he a dictator? Was he a tyrant? Did he love power for power's sake, or was he serving his country for the sake of his people? Did he have a "Mandarin's complex" and, if so, what did that mean? Was he honest? Did he have integrity of character? Was he his own man or the pawn of his family? What were his credentials to leadership? Did he really desire to develop democratic institutions? Was he right in opposing the Viet Cong, or had he, by arbitrary rule and neglect of his people, caused the Viet Cong to revolt? In short, should America continue to back South Vietnam under this man's leadership? I remembered, too, President Kennedy's remark before I left Washington a month before: "The outcome of your mission depends on what kind of man Diem is."

Arriving at two o'clock, I was greeted courteously by the Vietnamese President. None of his ministers was present. We sat down in a bright, pleasant room to become acquainted and, as it turned out, to discuss the beginning of a new and fateful chapter in Vietnamese-American relations.

We talked at length about Vietnamese history, about the different peoples of Vietnam and the problems they faced, about the task at hand as Diem saw it. Diem shared his ideas with me enthusiastically, stopping often for my questions and addressing them thoroughly. He laughed occasionally, sometimes at himself. In his youth he had not planned to go into government. He had studied theology but had concluded that political factors in Vietnam were more relevant than religious dogma, especially in a country where there were such various religions and sects. His older brother, Bishop Ngo Dinh Thuc, he told me, had called him "too unworldly for the Church." While a devout Christian, he came through to me as a Confucian, more interested in social relations and understanding than in a creed.

He called his country "sous-développé, sous-unifié et sous attaque" (underdeveloped, under-unified, and under attack). This turned out to be an apt description. I said that I thought our increased aid, as promised by Vice President Johnson, could help alleviate the first and third conditions. As to the second, it was up to him.

Diem took the point, agreeing that no foreign country could unify South Vietnam except by force and occupation. Effective internal political leadership was the only way. That was his mission and his goal. He felt that he had provided good leadership for six years, and he was encouraged by the results of his first term. At this beginning of his second term as President he felt that his mission was even more difficult because of the greatly increased Viet Cong insurgency. In answer to my questions, he attributed this increase to North Vietnam's change in tactics, propaganda, secret agents, and the infiltration of men and supplies to the Viet Cong. He was not discouraged, he said. With the moral and material support of friendly countries, he was ready to "begin again" the unification and pacification of his country.

When I left six hours later to join my wife and children before dinner, I felt that I had established real communication with this man. I had the impression of an extraordinary person, a man of much learning and many contradictions—dedicated, courteous, sincere, proud, suspicious, stubborn, but above all passionate in his conviction that the cause of a free Vietnam was worth any price, to himself and to all of his countrymen. I had by no means made up my mind about him, but I was impressed by one quality—his dedication. I began to feel that it would be possible to build the bridge of confidence between our two countries which was the cardinal point of my instructions from President Kennedy, and that it would be valuable to do so.

Two and one-half years later, Diem was overthrown and killed while the American press generally applauded and the U.S. government stood ready and eager to recognize his successors. Three weeks after that President Kennedy was slain in Dallas. For more than two years, I worked between these two men, trying to build the effective cooperation that both of them desired. Their national purposes were congruent: Diem's, to save his country from communism; Kennedy's, to show that America would not tolerate further subversive attacks on people who desired to be free. In temperament, background, and method the two leaders were, of course, vastly different. Despite these differences, I think that for two years our mission had remarkable success in building effective cooperation between them. In the end, however, when the crucial tests came, Kennedy gave way to the pressures of a misinformed public opinion, and Diem reverted to suspicion and mistrust.

This is the story of how these events appeared to me as I worked with other members of the U.S. Embassy in Saigon to help Vietnam achieve peace and freedom, and why still today I feel that by encouraging the revolt against Ngo Dinh Diem, the Kennedy administration set the stage for the tragedy that followed.

1

Background, 1946–1961

As background to this account, a brief history of America's earlier contacts with Vietnam may be of interest. In point of fact, America's direct influence on the Indo-China peninsula was marginal until several years after the end of World War II.

In 1946–47, as the opposition of the Vietminh to the return of French rule intensified, the United States, in spite of its traditional anticolonialism, was sympathetic to France.[2] There were two main reasons for this, which I cite without evaluation. France was a key factor in the recovery of Western Europe, and the loss of Indo-China, it was feared, would so weaken its centrist government as to lead to a political upheaval and possibly a Communist takeover in France itself. The other reason was the belief that a Vietminh victory would amount to the communization of Indo-China. Vietminh leader Ho Chi Minh was known to be a lifelong agitator and revolutionary, trained in Moscow in Leninist ideology and tactics. Whereas the United States regarded President Sukarno in nearby Indonesia as an indigenous nationalist, Ho Chi Minh, on the contrary, was viewed as a tool of Soviet-inspired world communism.

The United States urged France to support a non-Communist nationalist counterforce to the Vietminh, and in 1949 the quasi-independent government of Bao Dai was established. Installed by the French, Bao Dai's government had little popular support. At that time, another and more compelling reason was added for U.S. support of the anti-Communist forces in Indo-China—of which about three-quarters were native Vietnamese. This was Mao Tse-tung's stunning victory in China. General mobilization was decreed in Vietminh territory, and in February 1950, Vo Nguyen Giap, the Vietminh military leader, stated, "The covert war has ended and open warfare has begun." Moscow recognized Ho Chi Minh's government on February 1, 1950, and Communist China and Yugoslavia followed suit. Ho Chi Minh proclaimed in a broadcast, "Henceforth we definitely belong to the powerful anti-imperialist bloc of eight hundred million men." Chinese aid to the Vietminh—food, arms and ammunition, military advisors, and military training both in Vietnam and

China—began in March 1950. For its part, the United States decided to send material aid to France and its Vietnamese allies, beginning with the modest sums of $15 million for military aid and $25 million for economic assistance.

On June 25, 1950, the North Koreans struck in force across the 32nd parallel, and the Korean War began. For two years this limited but bloody war, involving Chinese as well as North Korean forces, served to divert American attention from Indo-China, where the Vietminh forces steadily strengthened. Whether planned or not, this was an example of the kind of reciprocal action in which the Communists are experts.

After the Korean War, U.S. aid to the French and the Associated States of Indo-China increased rapidly, until in 1954 we were paying 78 percent of the total cost of the war. The United States, however, had no part in the policies or conduct of the war at that stage—a fact which caused considerable friction between French and American representatives in Indo-China. Nevertheless, battle after battle was won by the French and their Associated States armies. The Vietminh countered with ambush after ambush. Casualties mounted. The French were losing more officers than were being graduated from St. Cyr, the French military academy. Neither side was winning a decisive victory.

After eight years of fighting, the French people lost heart in the struggle and elected Pierre Mendes-France premier on his promise to end the war in Indo-China. True to his word, Mendes-France called for negotiations, and the first Geneva Conference on Indo-China was convened in May 1954. The famous battle of Dien Bien Phu was fought and lost the day before the conference convened. Despite this resounding Vietminh victory and the consequent loss of French prestige, the relative military strengths of the two sides were not greatly affected. A compromise was agreed upon at the conference which was not unfavorable to freedom-loving Vietnamese, at least in a part of their native land.

The Geneva Accords of 1954 provided, among other things, for the cessation of hostilities, the independence and netural status of Vietnam, Cambodia, and Laos, and the temporary division of Vietnam at the 17th parallel pending a vote on unification. The armed forces of both sides were to be withdrawn to their respective territories, and neither side was to be reinforced from outside. Provision was also made for an exchange of civilians at their choice. Neither the government of South Vietnam (GVN) nor the United States signed the Accords, but the United States agreed not to violate them; and South Vietnam, under Ngo Dinh Diem, tacitly accepted them with one exception—the provision on unification.

After the withdrawal of the French Expeditionary Corps and the partitioning of Indo-China, all the world expected South Vietnam to stagger and fall quickly into the arms of Hanoi. This was also the consensus of the American press. Both halves of Vietnam, however, were beset by great difficulties and faced Herculean tasks of reconstruction and readjustment. To the surprise of most observers, progress toward order and economic stability proceeded faster in the South, despite the absorption of 900,000 refugees from the North, due in part to more abundant food supplies. It is noteworthy that Hanoi did not press at that time for unification as provided in the Geneva Accords. Ho Chi Minh had his hands full coping with internal problems, including a violent peasants' revolt, and was presumably as unsure about the outcome of a referendum as was President Diem. In any event, a period of relatively peaceful competition ensued between Hanoi and Saigon, as each leader strove by different means to bring order and a measure of economic viability into his shattered country. This was the beginning of the period that has been called "the miracle of Diem."

It was only in 1954, upon the withdrawal of the French, that direct American involvement in Vietnam began. During the next six years, South Vietnam, with American aid of about $150 million a year, accomplished a number of remarkable things. Rice production rose from 2.8 million metric tons to 4.6 million metric tons, and rubber production rose from 66,000 metric tons to over 79,000. Diversification of crops was encouraged, resulting in large increases in jute, kapok, copra, tea, coffee, fruit, and vegetables. New lands were opened for resettlement. By 1961, eighty agriculture extension agents were working in thirty-two provinces, and 575 4-T clubs (the Vietnamese version of 4-H clubs) with a membership of 20,681 rural boys and girls were active in 2,330 villages. Over 200,000 people had taken up new lands, each family receiving five hectares (about twelve acres), of which one hectare had been cleared by the government. The rest they cleared themselves. Nearly 1 million refugees from the North had been resettled in one way or another and enabled to become contributing members of society.

With government help, the commercial catch of fish rose from about 100,000 tons in 1955 to 250,000 tons in 1961. The government's farm credit program loaned over 3 billion piastres to over 1 million farm families. (In 1961 the exchange rate was seventy-three piastres to one U.S. dollar.) A national agricultural college was established with a membership of 110,000 and a paid-in capital of over 50 billion piastres.

This period also marked the beginning of an industrial base in a country which until then had had almost no industry whatsoever. Fifty-one manufacturing firms were established in South Vietnam between 1955 and 1961. The largest were textile plants, which attracted 560 million piastres in investments. New factories reduced imports of refined sugar from 25,000 metric tons in

1954 to zero in 1961. By manufacturing many of the things formerly imported, South Vietnam saved about $40 million annually in foreign exchange. For a small, impoverished country, this was not insignificant.

In transportation and communications, the railroad system was repaired, and by 1958 the line from Saigon to the demilitarized zone was operating for the first time in twelve years. Three major highways were completed, and others were under construction. Small landing fields for light aircraft dotted the country. Fourteen and one-half million cubic meters of infill were dredged from canals, restoring the water transport system in the Mekong Delta area. Electric power generation doubled.

In health measures, 3,500 hamlet health stations were established; training facilities for health workers were developed; the number of doctors graduating from medical school increased rapidly; and facilities were developed to train 120 professional nurses and 100 assistant nurses annually. In education, the number of students, teachers, and classrooms more than doubled in five years. Two new universities were established, one in Hue, in Central Vietnam, and one in Dalat. Four new technical vocational schools were opened. A government information program and library facilities were established in most of the forty-one provinces and in all the major cities.

To protect these economic and social developments from Viet Cong attacks, a native army of 350,000 men was raised, equipped, trained, and deployed. A civil guard for the protection of the peasants in the provinces was formed with American equipment and training. Police for the cities and rural police forces were established, equippped, and trained. These were major, difficult accomplishments.

Political reform accompanied economic and social reform. In 1955 South Vietnam drew up, ratified, and put into effect a constitution and a system of free national elections. This was a new concept of government for the Vietnamese people. That it did not work perfectly was no surprise, given Vietnam's age-old traditions of authoritarian government. The surprise was that it worked as well as it did. The constitution, modeled on that of the United States, provided for an elected president, vice president, and legislature, a cabinet of responsible ministers, and a supreme court. Ngo Dinh Diem was elected President in 1955 and again in 1961. Elections for the National Assembly were held regularly until October 1963. All this was done in a vigorous and, on the whole, successful effort to knit together a torn, confused, heterogeneous, and devastated country.

The U.S. role in this achievement was substantial in terms of moral and political support, economic and technical aid, and military supplies and training, amounting to about $150 million a year. President Diem's leadership, however, was credited as the major factor in the success.

In 1959, however, the Vietnamese Communists changed their tactics. Slowly, covertly, and subtly, a period of renewed aggression against the people of South Vietnam began. Alarmed by the progress in the South, and having gotten a firm grip on the North, Ho Chi Minh decided that Vietnam should be reunited, by force if necessary. Using the Geneva Accords of 1954 as a legal cover, he employed his ready tools—the Vietminh organizers, armed cadres, and sympathizers who were left behind with their weapons in the South after the Accords, or who had been taken to the North for indoctrination and training and surreptitiously sent back to their native villages in the South.

The Viet Cong's first objective was to undermine the government of the South, to set back or destroy what had been painfully built up by the Diem government over the past years. Their instruments were slander, propaganda, incitement of local grievances, promises, threats—working up to terror, bombings, kidnappings, and murders—reinforced at each stage by supplies and trained agents from North Vietnam. By 1961, their tactics of terror had created a grave stituation in South Vietnam. President Diem sent urgent appeals to the United States and other countries for material and moral support to help put down the insurgency. In Washington, this appeal was received with sympathy by the new administration. President Kennedy appointed a high-level Interdepartmental Task Force to consider it urgently.

2

Assignment to Vietnam

In the years following my entry into the U.S. Department of State in 1946, I served in a variety of positions in Washington and abroad, including that of Special Assistant to the Secretary of State for Mutual Security Affairs. When appointed to Vietnam at the beginning of 1961, I was Alternate U.S. Representative to the North Atlantic Council and deputy chief of the U.S. Mission to NATO, located at that time in Paris. I had been there since 1955.

Although most of my experience in Washington and abroad was in dealing with European countries, I had earlier spent several months in Japan and North China with a fellow student, and in 1953 I had a vivid glimpse of the Indo-China struggle when, as an assistant to Secretary of State John Foster Dulles, I heard Premier Pierre Mendes-France's last-ditch plea for U.S. naval and air support in the French war against the Viet Minh—a plea which the Eisenhower administration turned down. Since that time I had followed developments in Indo-China from afar, but with special interest. Nevertheless, I was surprised when, in the early days of the Kennedy administration., Secretary of State Dean Rusk asked me to go as Ambassador to Vietnam. Why I was selected for that post I do not know. The year before, during the Eisenhower administration, Secretary of State Christian Herter had asked me to go as Ambassador to Laos, a small country whose fate was of great concern to the Eisenhower administration. After some discussion, Secretary Herter withdrew his request, principally because my boss, Ambassador Randolph Burgess, strenuously urged that I remain at NATO.

Dean Rusk was one of the many people who left the armed forces and joined the State Department after World War II. I was another, having just been discharged from the Navy. In some cases, we worked together rather closely. I do not know for sure, but it is possible that my assignment to Vietnam was Rusk's idea. Whatever the reason for it, my nomination was one of several diplomatic appointments approved by the Senate Foreign Relations Committee on March 14, 1961, and later by the full Senate. I was not required to testify before the Committee. After fifteen years of service in the State

Department, my posting to Vietnam appeared to be a routine presidential appointment. I was gratified and honored by it.

Experience in the State Department had revealed to me no set pattern of how policy is made. Each administration developed its own method of decision-making. In the case of Vietnam in the first months of the Kennedy administration, a review and reappraisal of U.S. policy was undertaken by means of an Interdepartmental Task Force on Vietnam, which met in Washington. I was brought back from Paris in April 1961 to attend its meetings, and this constituted the major part of my briefing for my new assignment.

The Task Force was composed of people experienced and knowledgeable about Vietnam from several departments and agencies: the State Department, Defense, the Central Intelligence Agency, the White House, the Agency for International Development (AID), and the United States Information Agency (USIA). Its chairman was Deputy Secretary of Defense Roswell Gilpatric. I was among its least knowledgeable members, although I had read telegrams from Saigon and Washington that had been sent to Paris, had studied a number of officials reports on Vietnam, and had read many articles and several books on the subject. In Europe I also had the opportunity to talk with French and British officials, as well as others with long experience in Vietnam, including a number of Vietnamese nationals living in Paris. Most of the latter were voluntary exiles and anti-Diem in various degrees and for various reasons.

The Task Force on Vietnam met in the Pentagon. The principal question the Task Force examined was whether the United States should continue to support South Vietnam through the Diem governnment, which the U.S. had been doing since 1954. It seemed to me, even then, more of a political than a military problem—a problem to be treated from the beginning in a foreign policy context, with military participation and advice, but under the continuous leadership of the Department of State. Placing the Deputy Secretary of Defense in charge of the Task Force put too much military emphasis on Vietnam.

I commented on this to Secretary Rusk, who responded to the effect that he had had such a rough time on Laos that he would just as soon let the Pentagon take the lead on Vietnam. I was too new to the area, too excited about my new assignment, and too unwary of the pitfalls to make an issue of it. Years later, I asked Roswell Gilpatric why he had chaired the Task Force. He replied, "You're asking me? I don't know." He was assigned the task and in my opinion made an excellent chairman. In retrospect, however, the fact that this first Task Force was organized under the aegis of the Department of Defense had considerable symbolic as well as practical significance in Washington and in Saigon as time went on.

Perhaps the Task Force member I learned most from was Colonel, later

Brigadier General, Edward G. Lansdale, who had served during the 1950s in both the Philippines and Vietnam. Someone told me that this experience, as well as an extremely persuasive memorandum about Vietnam which Lansdale sent him, had caused President Kennedy to consider naming him Ambassador to Vietnam. But there had been some question of Lansdale's having been linked to undercover operations in the region, so the idea was dropped. Lansdale knew President Diem well. He had faith in him and spoke persuasively in favor of supporting the constitutionally elected government of Vietnam under Diem. I think he was one of the people who was most influential in persuading the Task Force that support for South Vietnam under Diem's leadership was a good risk in terms of U.S. interests. He did acknowledge that "there are a lot of criticisms that can be leveled against this government in South Vietnam, but compared to others in Southeast Asia, it's a beaut," or words to that effect.

The members of the Task Force were realistic about the situation in Vietnam. They realized the implacability of the Communist movement in Vietnam and throughout the region and recognized the inherent instability in South Vietnam since the division of the country by the Geneva Accords in 1954. They looked upon South Vietnam in much the same terms as the United States regarded West Germany and South Korea—as the best solution obtainable (temporary or possibly permanent) to the problem of containing Communist expansion throughout the world, short of another major war. They took seriously the recognition of the Republic of South Vietnam by the United States in 1954 as an independent country, followed by eighteen other formal recognitions. They knew the hazards and the stakes involved in supporting South Vietnam. These were basics accepted by the Task Force from the previous administration.

New factors included the following. The Viet Cong had recently increased their insurgency, dangerously undermining the progress South Vietnam had achieved since 1954. The killing of government officials in the provinces was indicative. Nearly 2,400 civil servants were killed or abducted by the Viet Cong in 1960. The Diem government had been unable to protect them or to carry on its improvements in many areas. Some reservations were expressed about the staying power of the United States against the Communists' determination. On the whole, though, it was felt that in a divided Southeast Asia, and particularly in South Vietnam, a large majority of the people were anti-Communist. They hated the Viet Cong's brutality. Most Task Force members were aware that the United States could not expect a clear-cut decision in Vietnam in a short while, and that this was the kind of situation with which the impatient American public and the volatile American political situation were ill equipped to cope.

In spite of the fact that the Eisenhower administration had become dissatisfied with the government of South Vietnam under President Diem, the Kennedy Task Force reached a consensus that Diem was the most promising leader available and that U.S. support of South Vietnam under his elected government would be in our national interest. In effect, it favored a fresh start in our relations with the Diem government and stronger American support. I do not recall any dissents to this conclusion.

The Task Force devoted its attention almost exclusively to Vietnam. The closely related problems of the rest of Indo-China—in particular Laos and Cambodia—were not extensively treated. In retrospect, this must be considered an error of great consequence, for it became apparent soon enough that the interlocking problems of Indo-China could not successfully be dealt with separately. In Washington, the planning for the Indo-China area in 1961 was piecemeal, while our Communist adversaries, I soon found out, regarded the Indo-China peninsula as one strategic area and did their planning accordingly. This point was well illustrated by the new administration's vacillation over how to handle the problem of Laos in March 1961. President Kennedy had first appeared on TV to announce a strong military stand against the Communist insurgents in that country, but he soon reversed himself and opted for a diplomatic solution—a negotiated settlement aimed at creating a neutral state. The Communist planners, looking at the region as a strategic whole, could see advantages in negotiating about Laos while building up their strength in South Vietnam. They did not fail to take into account the relationship between the two situations.

Kennedy's Task Force did not go deeply into the history of Vietnam or into the seven-year period of U.S. support of South Vietnam under the Eisenhower administration. This was a new and self-assured administration, looking forward to new accomplishments. It was more activist, more confident, and less cautious than its predecessor. At the time, I shared the prevailing attitude set forth in President Kennedy's eloquent Inaugural Address. But since that ringing speech, things had not gone well. The U.S. invasion of Cuba at the Bay of Pigs was an admitted disaster, encouraging the Soviet Union to exert more pressure on the United States in Europe and elsewhere. Chairman Nikita Khrushchev openly proclaimed his policy of supporting "wars of national liberation" and tried to bully our young President at their first meeting in Vienna. The issue over Berlin had become critical again, threatening nuclear war. The showdown victory of the administration at the time of the Cuban missile crisis had not yet occurred. There was anxiety in the air and a strong determination to come back from reversals.

It was in this atmosphere that the Task Force on Vietnam made its report to President Kennedy in April 1961, about the time of my departure to Saigon.

It recommended a positive but limited response to the urgent South Vietnamese request for more aid. Citing the progress made under President Diem since 1955 and the role of American assistance in that accomplishment, it proposed positive measures to counter the recent resurgence of Viet Cong violence. It recommended deeper and more consistent American cooperation with the Republic of Vietnam to help the Vietnamese restore order, resume their economic and social progress, and determine their political future without coercion. It called for increased American aid in the form of military and police equipment and training, technical and economic assistance, and a much wider and deeper role in advising the Vietnamese on the effective use of our aid. This was to be accomplished by establishing a relationship of *confidence* at all levels between our mission in Saigon and those we dealt with in the government of South Vietnam. As under the Eisenhower administration, the use of American combat forces was not envisioned at that time.

These conclusions were wrapped up in the guidelines for my new mission, which were cleared throughout the government. President Kennedy approved them. They were, in effect, our overall instructions throughout my tenure as Ambassador in Saigon. The goal of the Kennedy policy remained essentially the same as under the Eisenhower administration, namely, to assist South Vietnam to strengthen itself and to defend itself against subversion. The strength of this commitment differed, however. In view of the additional pressures the South Vietnamese were under because of Viet Cong activity and Hanoi's increased support of it, the United States would provide more material aid and training to South Vietnam, through its elected government, and greater moral support.

The policy also differed in its approach to the Diem government. My predecessor, Elbridge Durbrow, had gone to President Diem in an attempt to have Diem's brother, Ngo Dinh Nhu, transferred out of Saigon as an ambassador to some other country. Acting on instructions from the Eisenhower administration, which had become concerned about Nhu's influence, Ambassador Durbrow's demarche was forceful. It was coldly received. There was friction on other matters as well, so that by the spring of 1961 Diem had grown suspicious of the United States' motives toward South Vietnam. This was why the Task Force report emphasized the need to establish a new relationship of mutual confidence between the two governments.

Vietnam was to be the site of the Kennedy administration's stand against communism in Southeast Asia, the answer to Khrushchev's threat of nibbling wars of national liberation. Initially, the President had publicly designated Laos the scene for this contest of wills. Some policymakers, however, felt that Laos, whose location and terrain made it practically inaccessible, was the last place in Southeast Asia where the United States ought to make a stand. The administration therefore decided to work for a negotiated settlement in Laos and to increase its help to defend South Vietnam. In 1961, the decision was *not* that the United States would get involved in terms of combat forces, but rather that we would help South Vietnam defend itself more successfully by increased aid, advice, training, and diplomatic support.

It was the Task Force report that prompted President Kennedy's remark to me about the importance he attached to finding out what kind of man President Diem was—for even then, after seven years of Diem's leadership of South Vietnam and of American aid and moral support to his country, he was an engima to most Americans. The Task Force in Washington had focused on the quality of Diem's government and in particular on the character of the man himself. I noted certain differences of view. Some members were inclined to judge the Vietnamese government by its progress in developng Western-style democratic institutions. Others with more experience in the Far East focused attention on the government's ability to pacify the country and to provide essential government services to the people. Regarding President Diem himself, I noted that those who knew him best seemed to respect him most.

Although the Task Force's consensus was that Diem was the best available leader for South Vietnam, I was determined to make up my own mind about him. In this I was encouraged by our new President. Kennedy also stressed that he wanted the mission in Saigon to be unified, with overall authority and responsibility centered in the Ambassador. He later reiterated these instructions in directives to all missions of a similar type. I found the President well informed, hopeful, and vigorous about Vietnam.

On the morning of my swearing-in at the State Department, I received a call from the Under Secretary of State, Chester Bowles, who said that a last-minute switch was being considered. Kenneth Young, recently appointed as Ambassador to Thailand, might be sent to South Vietnam and I to Thailand, because Young knew Diem personally through his business experience in Southeast Asia, and I had experience in NATO (and presumably therefore knew the workings of SEATO, headquartered in Bangkok). That idea might have had some logic, but the hour was late, and Young and I were briefed and ready to go. Bowles' suggestion was not approved. I was glad at the time.

The Secretary of State, Dean Rusk, certainly did not appear to foresee a prolonged American involvement in Vietnam when I called to say good-bye. In fact, Rusk was surprisingly gloomy about the prospects of South Vietnam's retaining its independence. Toward the end of our discussion, I mentioned to him that for reasons of our children's education and other family needs, it was important for me to know the duration of my assignment. One of our daughters was already in college in the States, another would enter in the fall, while the younger two were to go with us to Saigon and attend school there. In a couple of years, these two would also need to be back in the United States for school or college. We did not want our children cut off from our family life for too long a period. I had discussed this with some of Rusk's subordinates, and we had concluded that a two-year tour of duty seemed about right. I hoped the Secretary of State would agree. To my surprise, Rusk said, "You don't have to worry about the length of your stay. The way things are going out there, we'll be lucky if we still have a mission in Saigon six months from now." Rusk's pessimism may explain his reluctance to have the State Department take the lead in the Vietnam problem at that time. His remark was not encouraging, but at least it gave me reason to think that he would recall our conversation at a later date.

3

In Harness

As is not unusual in the Foreign Service, our departure to Saigon on May 5, 1961, was somewhat precipitous. President Kennedy had decided to send Vice President Johnson on a quick trip to the Far East especially to observe and report on South Vietnam, and it was deemed necessary for me to be there "in harness" before the Vice President and his party arrived. Accordingly, my wife, three of our daughters, and I left Washington in a hurry.

We had a brief stopover in Honolulu, where I conferred with my friend and predecessor, Elbridge Durbrow. Not surprisingly, Durbrow was most informative and helpful during our meeting, despite his recent estrangement from President Diem. He felt, I believe, that his disagreements with the government of South Vietnam were minor compared to the overall need to establish stability there.

In talks with Admiral Harry D. "Don" Felt, Commander-in-Chief of U.S. Forces in the Pacific, headquartered in Honolulu, I found much encouragement, based on his knowledge of Vietnam and of President Diem. Admiral Felt made frequent trips to Saigon and was on close terms with Diem.

My family and I arrived in Saigon on May 9. It was necessary for me to have a white sharkskin suit, the diplomatic rig in Saigon, in order to present my credentials to the President of the Republic, thus getting "into harness." A tailor was found who had the material and made the suit overnight. The next day, I presented my credentials at the "Independence Palace." This was a fine building with a deer park and high fence; it was built by the French to house the Governor General and was taken over by the Vietnamese government after the French left. At the brief ceremony, my credentials were politely accepted by a stout, short man in his late fifties, with coal-black hair; he also wore a white sharkskin suit. His ministers stood behind him in respectful silence, some of them in traditional Vietnamese garb.

Vice President and Mrs. Johnson arrived the following day. They were guests of President Ngo Dinh Diem. Diem's sister-in-law, Madame Ngo Dinh Nhu, was the official hostess, Diem being a bachelor. The Johnsons were accom-

panied by a group of officials from Washington, including members of the
Kennedy family, Mr. and Mrs. Stephen Smith. This touch was not lost on the
Ngo family. Jean Kennedy and Stephen Smith's presence indicated to them
that the Kennedy administration appreciated strong family ties, and, unlike
its predecessor, did not want to divorce President Diem from his family.

The Vice President's visit was symbolic on another level. No American
official of such importance had been in Vietnam since Vice President Nixon's
visit in 1957. Furthermore, Johnson was visiting Vietnam at President Kennedy's request. Thus the visit emphasized the determination with which the
Kennedy administration intended to support South Vietnam's independence.

Mr. Johnson spent four whirlwind days in Vietnam. There were conferences
with President Diem and his advisors, followed by inspection trips in and
around Saigon, receptions, public appearances, dinners, and more conferences. The Vice President spoke strongly on the need to maintain a free
Vietnam. Both publicly and privately he was forthright and cordial in his
dealings with President Diem, his family, and his government. As a participant,
I was impressed by Mr. Johnson's drive and energy, by President Diem's calm
determination and inner force, and especially by the enormous differences
of approach to political leadership between the two men—the one Occidental
and the other Oriental, the one outgoing and the other reserved, the one
seeking popular approval and the other seeking to deserve respect, the one
democratic in our sense, the other paternalistic in his attitude toward his
people, in the accepted Mandarin tradition. Yet there was an evident rapport
between them.

An amusing aspect of Vice President Johnson's visit developed from his
vigorous "campaigning" on behalf of Vietnamese democracy. As we toured
Saigon and its environs, crowds—some of which I am sure were drummed
up by the government—would gather where he was going to stop. Mr. Johnson would plunge into the crowd, shaking hands and greeting people, much
as he might have done during a political campaign in Johnson City, Texas.
This in itself was no mean achievement, for the Vietnamese people were not
accustomed to shaking hands. Their customary mode of greeting in 1961,
before Americanization had taken hold, was to press the palms of their hands
together in front and bow. But they are quick to learn and eager to please;
people were soon reaching out to Johnson, and even holding out their babies.
After the Vice President's departure, an informal "Shake the Hand Lyndon
Johnson Club" developed, composed of men, women, and children who
claimed to have shaken Mr. Johnson's hand. He had indeed shaken many
hands, but practically whole towns would claim membership. Between stops
the Vice President, sweating profusely in the very hot climate, would change
his shirt in the back of our car. Of course, when we arrived at the next stop,

his shirt would be wet again. This did not, however, appear to deter people from joining the "Shake the Hand Lyndon Johnson Club."

At the farewell dinner given for him on a very hot evening just before the monsoon rains began, Vice President Johnson responded to President Diem's toast in unforgettable terms. He spoke of President Kennedy's wish to establish firm and understanding relations between our two countries and governments. That, he said, was why he was sent by President Kennedy to Vietnam. He praised Diem for his strong and unwavering resolve to protect his hard-pressed country from Communist domination and promised increased American moral and material support to the government and people of South Vietnam. Then, shifting to more familiar ground, he referred with glowing admiration to Diem's election results at the polls a month before. In some countries, he said, politicians are content with 55 percent of the votes, or even less, but "your people, Mr. President, returned you to office for a second term with 91 percent of the votes. You are not only the George Washington, the Father of your country, but the Franklin Roosevelt as well." At the end of this extraordinary eulogy, on a signal from Mr. Johnson, we all rose and drank a toast in warm champagne to the President of the Republic of Vietnam.

The same enthusiasm was reflected in the joint communiqué issued to the press at the end of Vice President Johnson's visit. Usually these statements are rather flat documents that very politely say nothing. But this one strongly declared U.S. support for South Vietnam and implied that America would increase this support if necessary.[3] I had assisted Vice President Johnson in drafting the communiqué, which was worded more strongly that I would have done on my own at the time. After we sent the statement for approval to Washington, Mr. Johnson retired, requesting that I notify him when the reply arrived.

I remember sitting up until four or five o'clock in the morning waiting for Washington's answer. About 4 A.M., Saigon time, there came a telegram followed by a telephone call from Washington, suggesting even stronger language for one section of the communiqué. I asked my assistant, who, with a communications officer, was the only person with me at the Embassy at that hour, to telephone the Vice President, making sure to put me on the line first. A few moments later I got a buzz on the intercom: "The Vice President is coming on the line." To my surprise, I found myself speaking not to Lyndon Johnson but to the Vice President of South Vietnam, Nguyen Ngoc Tho, whom I had met the day before. I said, "I beg your pardon, Mr. Vice President. I was trying to get my own Vice President." Tho laughed and said, "It is a rather unusual time to call." Vice President Johnson, when I reached him, enthusiastically approved the strengthened communiqué.

Whether the "meet the people" demonstration of popular democracy that

Mr. Johnson put on in Saigon had any effect on President Diem's political style is doubtful. I did raise the matter with Diem later, after getting to know him better. While he showed good humor and a certain curiosity about American politicians' practices, he concluded with a serious remark: "There are profound differences between the Vietnamese and American people, in customs, outlook, political training, and philosophy. I hope we can find a bridge between Eastern and Western cultures." But Diem did not miss the opportunity of reminding me of Johnson's remark about his getting 91 percent of the vote.

In another toast during his visit, Vice President Johnson compared President Diem to Andrew Jackson and Woodrow Wilson. I did not quite get the relevance of this, but I remember it distinctly. A few days later, when Diem was showing me some architectural plans he had drawn for the Vietnamese Army Cadet School at Dalat, I remarked that our Vice President should have included Thomas Jefferson, the architect, in the list of famous presidents to whom he had likened President Diem. Diem responded with a twinkle that while he was flattered by Mr. Johnson's remarks, he felt that they may have been a little *de trop*. But he also expressed warm appreciation for the lift given to Vietnamese morale by the Vice President's visit.

It was a week later that President Diem invited me to join him at Dalat to go over all of the things that had been discussed with the Vice President and the group that had accompanied him. Diem wanted a good block of time in which we could discuss these matters and develop a working plan on the cooperative effort between our two countries involving additional U.S. aid. As I have mentioned, this was also the first opportunity we had had to speak privately and thus for each of us really to assess the other.

The problem of communication with President Diem, of understanding not only the words but what lay behind them, and of being similarly understood, was uppermost in my mind as I drove to my two o'clock appointment with him at Dalat. I know of no greater pitfall than to rely entirely on interpreters, and I was determined to establish a direct and meaningful channel of communication with the Vietnamese President. Fortunately, he agreed with me, and at that meeting we spoke in French without interpreters. If one of us did not understand the other, he would stop him and ask him to repeat or clarify the point. We followed this pattern during the next two and one-half years. Of course, if there were visitors present and it was to be a three- or four-way exchange, we would have an interpreter. But in our face-to-face conversations we used none.

I soon became aware of one of President Diem's personal idiosyncracies about which I had heard from my predecessor—his incredible verbosity. Our first conversation lasted six hours. Actually, it did not seem nearly so long, for I found the subjects we discussed fascinating. Diem led off with his interpretation of Vietnamese history, from the ancient past, through the Chinese wars, the French occupation, the Japanese conquest, and the confused aftermath of World War II. His richly documented survey of the Vietnamese people, their origins, their culture, and their destiny started before the Christian era and ended, not in the present, but several centuries in the future. It was presented by a man obviously obsessed by the need to explain to me—and through me to my government—his raison d'être, which was nothing less than to save his country once again from an alien culture, coming this time in the garb of communism.

I had read some Vietnamese history, I knew about its wars for independence, and I had heard of Diem's depth of penetration into a subject. Fortunately, I had a considerable background of philosophy and comparative religion. But I was not prepared for anything like this. I listened with growing interest. I asked questions. Each question opened up a whole new chapter, and after a while I began to realize the dedication and passion of this man, who had devoted his life to the preservation of his people's historic identity, as he understood and loved it.

Diem was a chain-smoker. Between us, we must have smoked several packs of Vietnamese cigarettes and drunk dozens of cups of pale, lukewarm Vietnamese tea. After our talk, President Diem joined Madame Nhu and her children, my wife and me, and our daughters for dinner at his brother's house in Dalat. It was a congenial evening. Ngo Dinh Nhu was away on a hunting trip, but Madame Nhu was charming and hospitable, as were her children. I particularly remember the Nhus' younger son, Quyen, playing Mozart on the piano before dinner. He was not yet ten, but he played very well, even though he could not reach the pedals. I also remember the informality with which we learned to use chopsticks and the ease of breaking protocol when after dinner it seemed time to go home. As we suspected, the President was courteously waiting for Madame Nhu's foreign guests to leave before he returned to his villa. His working days began at four in the morning, and he generally retired early

From this first talk, I began to see the roots of Vietnam's problems and its strange complexities, and to realize how difficult it would be to interpret them to my own government and people. I also began to feel that I would be working with a man of integrity, with whom it would be hard to come to specific agreements but who, once agreements were reached, could be counted upon to fulfill them. I was impressed by his sincerity and his apparent complete devotion to the cause of a free Vietnam. But I cautioned myself not to reach conclusions too quickly. Even though the very strong joint communiqué had been issued and the United States, through Vice President

Johnson, had gone all out in support of the government and its stand against the Viet Cong, I felt an obligation to take another look at the situation in Vietnam and to determine for myself whether support for the Diem government was in the United States' best interests.

In Saigon, I held individual meetings with my colleagues, sounding them out about the viability of the Diem government and getting their views on how to proceed. Our Embassy had representatives from almost every U.S. government agency and department dealing with foreign affairs. In addition to the State Department, we had representatives from the International Cooperation Administration (later to become the Agency for International Development), the Central Intelligence Agency, the United States Information Agency, the Defense Department's Military Assistance Advisory Group (MAAG), as well as Army, Navy, and Air Force attachés. The representatives of the Central Intelligence Agency worked under the cover of these other organizations. Although these people reported through their respective heads to their own agencies in Washington, it was my job as Ambassador to ensure that the work that came out of our mission supported U.S. policy toward Vietnam as defined by our instructions, and to work out any conflicts in the implementation of these instructions. This is what President Kennedy had meant when he told me he wanted a "unified mission" in Saigon. I exercised this same responsibility over our consulate in Hue.

The mission was at that time divided on the subject of the Diem regime. Joseph Mendenhall, the Embassy's Counselor for Political Affairs, was frankly negative. Mendenhall was chargé (acting head) of the Embassy when I arrived because the Deputy Chief of Mission, Francis Cunningham, was away on leave. (I had been told before leaving Washington that Cunninhgam was due to leave Saigon, and he was transferred soon after my arrival.) Mendenhall had been in Vietnam since August 1959 and was disillusioned with both President Diem and his government. He told me that he doubted President Diem's ability either to bring peace to South Vietnam or to serve its people effectively. He thought Diem was too autocratic and inefficient, although he did not question his honesty and sincerity.

I worked with Mendenhall for nearly a year and found that the longer he was in Vietnam, the more he doubted Diem's qualifications as President. Although I came to disagree with his views, I respected him—not the least because he was frank with me. After Mendenhall was transferred to Washington, he wrote to me from the National War College, which he was attending. He stated that he was going to write his thesis on an alternative to the Diem government and wanted to know if I had any objections or suggestions. I thought it was very fair of him to let me know about this and replied that if he thought he could develop a better alternative, then he should go ahead with his study. I certainly had no objections and would be interested in seeing the final product. As I recall, his study concluded that a military regime would be the best government for South Vietnam. He did not recommend a coup, but the government he envisioned was like the one that suceeded the Diem government after the 1963 overthrow.

John Anspacher and Arthur Gardiner were two other Embassy officers who were less than enchanted with the Diem regime. Like Mendenhall, both were members of the Embassy's overall Task Force, or Country Team. Anspacher, the Counselor for Public Affairs, had his doubts about Diem but did his best to support U.S. policy in Vietnam. He had been in Saigon for a little over a year. Gardiner was the Counselor for Economic Affairs and thus head of the large, active U.S. Operations Mission (USOM). He had been in the country since February 1958. Arthur was an old friend, and I suspect that, rather than being anti-Diem, he was disillusioned and disheartened. He had worked very hard and ably and felt that the Vietnamese economy should have responded better to the infusions of money it was receiving, as well as to his and the USOM's efforts in training and advice.

William Colby was another old Vietnam hand. Listed officially as First Secretary in the Embassy Political Section, he was really CIA Station Chief, head of CIA operations in Vietnam. Colby became not only a friend, but one of my most trusted advisors. One of the ablest members of our Embassy Task Force, he had also served in April as an advisor to the Interagency Task Force in Washington. Despite the doubts of some of his peers and some members of the Vietnamese armed forces, Bill Colby had confidence in our policy and programs. He conferred often with Ngo Dinh Nhu, President Diem's brother and political counselor, about specific CIA operations and the need for them. President Diem trusted and admired Colby, as I did.

The Embassy, of course, worked closely with the U.S. Military Assistance Advisory Group, headed by Lieutenant General Lionel McGarr. I found McGarr a fine person and a first-class military man. He had a difficult and demanding role as soldier-diplomat. One of his duties—on Department of Defense instructions, I am sure, but out of personal conviction as well—was to keep President Diem from interfering in the military operations of the South Vietnamese Army. He could be rather blunt with the Vietnamese President regarding this matter. Sometimes Diem would say to me, "General McGarr has been telling me again not to interfere, and I'm trying to let the military run their affairs, but I have to supervise." Diem thought highly of McGarr, however, and I think McGarr respected Diem and his administration. For my part, I still retain high regard for General McGarr.

Another excellent officer, Major General Charles Timmes, served as McGarr's second in command, before succeeding him as head of MAAG. A kind of military jack-of-all-trades, Charlie Timmes had an excellent touch with the Vietnamese, both military and civilian. He accomplished a great deal, particularly in the area of military advice and training, and was in all respects a fine colleague.

These were the key players I found in Saigon in the summer of 1961—our Country Team. They were the people with whom I worked and upon whom I relied to implement our instructions. From them and their subordinates—both in Saigon and in the field—I received much of the information that was reported regularly, along with my own observations, to our government in Washington.

Our job did not stop in Saigon, or at Vietnam's borders; we also worked in coordination with other U.S. embassies in Southeast Asia. For example, claims of border violations and other aspects of Vietnamese-Cambodian relations were recurring problems. The Parrot's Beak, an area jutting out toward Saigon, had been given to Cambodia as part of the 1954 Geneva Accords. The Vietnamese people never really accepted this, pointing out that this was not so on the old maps and claiming that the area's inhabitants were Vietnamese rather than Khmer. The territory involved was not large, but strategically important. It was used by the Viet Cong as a safe haven when they got into trouble in military actions.

Cambodia at that time was ruled by Prince Norodom Sihanouk, a neutralist, who had no interest in the struggle within Vietnam. There was no love lost between the Vietnamese and the Cambodians historically. Periodically the Cambodian government would claim that the Vietnamese had violated their borders or had mistreated Khmer minorities in Vietnamese towns. Frequently, the South Vietnamese government would claim the opposite. Because of these border disputes, William C. Trimble, U.S. Ambassador to Cambodia, and I would meet in Phnom Penh or in Saigon to discuss our mutual problems. We exchanged views and information, trying to promote some measure of cooperation between the neighboring countries, but we never resolved the age-old frictions between them. My discussions with Kenneth Young, U.S. Ambassador to Thailand, were more useful. The governments in Bangkok and Saigon saw the Communist threat to Southeast Asia in much the same light.

Our mission in Saigon was, of course, constantly in touch with Washington. We were its hands and voice, working with the South Vietnamese government to explain and implement the Kennedy administration's policies and programs to help them. We were also Washington's eyes and ears, observing, analyzing, and reporting on the Vietnamese political, social, and economic environment, on its ups and downs in controlling and pacifying the country, and especially on any developments that might affect U.S. policy. Our Task Force reports, usually drawn up in meetings over the weekend and telegraphed to Washington on Monday, represented the consensus of the Country Team. We tried to be objective, sometimes sending dissents as well, although I did exercise the privilege of commenting on the latter.[4]

I sent my reports to Washington through regular Department of State channels, rarely, if ever, making use of the CIA and Defense facilities available to me. Because of the nature of my relationship with General McGarr and later with General Paul Harkins and Bill Colby, I think I saw most, if not all, of the important cables sent through their channels.

In Washington, the Embassy's cables were received in the State Department's Bureau of Far Eastern Affairs, headed at the time by Assistant Secretary of State Walter McConaughy. Under his direction, the Department sent us good and helpful advice, and our mission received strong support and understanding from Sterling Cottrell, who headed the Vietnam Task Force in State. Our reports were distributed as appropriate throughout State, Defense, the White House, and elsewhere in the government. What we lacked most in Saigon during that first year (1961) was an efficient means of coordination with the government of Vietnam.

Mindful of President Kennedy's personal instruction to gauge what kind of leader President Diem was, and conscious of my responsibility to determine the degree of support for Diem, I toured the country extensively, not only the cities, but also the countryside. By the end of 1961 I had visited all of Vietnam's major cities and somewhere between thirty-five and thirty-eight of its forty-one provinces. Sometimes I went with President Diem and sometimes independently or with one of his cabinet officers. I tried to determine how the people reacted to him and his government and how that government served them.

From these trips I gained some insight into the psychology of the people. Vietnam is an ancient and beautiful region with a long, proud history. The people of Vietnam, North and South, are akin to the Chinese in culture and family traditions. Their ancient literature and plays, their Confucian outlook on life, even their language (transliterated in the seventeenth century from Chinese characters by Alexandre de Rhodes), are of Chinese origin. Unlike the Cambodians, whose culture and blood were strongly infused from India, and the Laotians, who were more immune from foreign influences because of their mountainous terrain, the Vietnamese people can be described as independent-minded relations of the great Chinese people. That they are independent-minded is attested by their recorded history, which can be summed up as 2,000 years of struggle against Chinese domination.

On the Gulf of Siam, in western South Vietnam, there was an archeological excavation which I once visited with President Diem. This was a Roman trading-post, where the Romans brought goods by ship to exchange for silks and spices brought overland by caravans. The post had a small forum, many carved statues, and relics of a rather extensive Roman colony. It gave one a sense of Vietnam's history, of which President Diem, like most Vietnamese, was extremely proud. Today this relic of history may be only a bomb crater—I do not know. But to me, visiting it in 1961, it depicted the survivability of the Vietnamese people. Their pride in their country and its traditions was everywhere evident, especially among the peasants. So was their longing for peace and security.

The boost to Vietnamese morale in 1961 created by American and other support, particularly Australian, was sorely needed, for Viet Cong terorism was taking its toll. I was a near-victim of assassination in Saigon in mid-July, when two youths on a motorbike threw a hand-grenade into the car in which I was riding. Fortunately, the grenade was a dud, and no one was hurt. I tried to downplay the incident, feeling that it would serve the Viet Cong's purposes if it received a lot of attention, thus making targets of other Americans in Vietnam. The young man who had actually thrown the bomb was caught, and I went to President Diem and asked him not to make an example of this youth because a foreign diplomat was involved. Diem agreed with my reasoning but explained that it would be difficult to comply in this case, since the young man had two weeks earlier thrown a grenade into a jeep and killed three South Vietnamese soldiers. Even so, the mission continued to play down the incident, as well as other attacks on Americans that occurred in July.

Shortly after this, Ambassador Ramchundur Goburdhun, the Indian Chairman of the UN-appointed International Control Commission to supervise compliance with the 1954 Geneva Accords, visited North Vietnamese Prime Minister Pham Van Dong in Hanoi. He told me that he had berated Dong for allowing or ordering his Viet Cong agents in Saigon to do something as stupid as trying to kill the U.S. Ambassador. The Prime Minister said he was sorry—it was a stupid thing to do, and he would try to see that it didn't happen again. This account puzzled me. Did Pham Van Dong mean that it was stupid to provoke the United States by such an act? Did he mean that Hanoi didn't have close control over the Viet Cong terrorists? Or was he simply trying to placate the Chairman of the International Control Commission? I suspect that all three factors were involved in Pham Van Dong's reply. It was significant, however, that the North Vietnamese Prime Minister did not deny Hanoi's connection with the Viet Cong.

Today terrorism, assassinations, and threats are commonplace in many parts of the world. We have almost become inured to them. In Vietnam, twenty-five or more years ago, such techniques had one of their early testing grounds. Threats of assassination were a constant part of life in Vietnam and were often carried out. After General Harkins and his wife arrived in 1962, he and I kept a scorecard of the threats of assassination received by each of us each week. I had the advantage over him because of my more numerous family (our wives and children were often threatened), but I remember feeling a sense of humiliation when, one week, he went ahead of me in this dismal game.

Out in the provinces, the terrorism increased in 1961. I visited a village where murdered men had been hung like scarecrows, warnings to the peace-loving people who lived there. In September, I visited a province adminis-tered by a vigorous, well-motivated young province chief. The next week the Viet Cong over ran his village, took him prisoner, and beheaded him in front of his wife and several small children. I have often wondered if there was any connection between my visit and his murder. He was, however, just one of the many South Vietnamese civilian government officials assassinated by the Viet Cong. The victims were for the most part minor officials, carrying on the government's work in the provinces, villages, and hamlets—agriculture extension agents, road engineers, dredge foremen, district chiefs, school teachers and supervisors, doctors and nurses, members of the antimalaria teams, land reform agents, postmen. The drain on the South Vietnamese government's human resources was indeed intolerable, and I wondered how such a small country could continue to replenish the ranks of its civil service.

The safest civil servants were invariably the worst ones. Since the Viet Cong objective was to paralyze the government in the provinces, nullify its services, and cut off the rural areas from contact with Saigon, government employees who did little or nothing were left unmolested. The active and conscientious ones, however, were singled out for threats, abduction, and murder, often with their wives and children. Yet, in spite of the risks, volunteers for gov-ernment jobs were plentiful.

Despite Viet Cong threats and violence, or perhaps because of them, from my travels throughout South Vietnam I grew to believe that the majority of the people, particularly the peasants in the provinces and the villages, were anti-Communist. I met village elders, bonzes in the pagodas, province chiefs, other lesser officials, farmers. Naturally, there were "fence sitters," especially in areas where Viet Cong terrorism was strongest or where close relatives of a family had joined the Viet Cong. But equally, I saw many cases of staunch-ness and courage among villagers vulnerable to Viet Cong attack, people who had little hope of quick support from government forces. My observations also led me to feel that a large majority of the South Vietnamese people resented the Viet Cong, respected President Diem, and in this sense supported his regime.

American reporters on these trips would often note what they termed a "lack of enthusiasm" for President Diem. I think the reporters misinterpreted what the marks of support were. Popularity in the Western democratic sense had no real meaning to the Vietnamese peasants. What they looked for in their leader was honesty and justice. If he provided that, he gained their respect. This was deeply ingrained from their Confucian heritage.

Instead of a lot of cheering and handclapping for the President, there was evident respect and a desire to talk about local problems with him or his representatives. It was not in the Vietnamese nature to hold big political demonstrations, but the people did want to talk about getting their rice to market, where and how they were being molested by the Viet Cong, and where the canals and bridges needed repair. They wanted to talk about schools and how to defend against the threats and atrocities against the school teachers. They wanted to know more about land reform and about everything from fertilizer for rice growing to building fish ponds. President Diem was especially interested in promoting the development of fish ponds. The fish raised in the muddy ponds were often the villagers' greatest source of protein. Diem encouraged pond construction, putting government money into it if he had local support. He understood the peasants and their needs better than he understood the people in Saigon, and vice versa.

From my observations of Diem and his government, I concluded that he was an honest and dedicated man, working in a very difficult situation with the best people he could get to help him. I agreed with his philosophy and aims. Diem was sincerely concerned with trying to bridge the gap between the mores, customs, and traditions of his own people and those of the West, with trying to put together the best parts of both. He was very much concerned with the welfare of his people, and with deeper philosophical problems of government, as well as with the urgent problem of survival against the Viet Cong.

There were, of course, many weaknesses in the Diem government. Diem himself was not a good administrator, although he was a terrifically hard and conscientious worker. He was inept in the handling of public relations, as were most of his advisors. He found it difficult, if not impossible, to delegate authority. In this he may not have been entirely at fault, for many Vietnamese officials were unwilling to take responsibility. There had not been a strong native civil service under France, and most of the South Vietnamese civil servants had been inherited from the French regime. They were often more concerned with keeping their jobs than with rolling up their sleeves and applying themselves to their duties. This was a constant source of worry for President Diem and his top officials, as it was to us. Sometimes our people in the field came upon cases of graft and corruption. President Diem was quite willing to look into these matters when we brought them to his attention, and, where he found the reports to be true, he would fire the person involved and hire someone else. Unfortunately, there was not an inexhaustible pool of good people to draw upon, and the shortage of able civil servants was exacerbated by the Viet Cong attacks against them.

Overall, however, I became convinced that the Diem regime was the best available to govern South Vietnam, and that it could and would improve. Thus I reported back to the Department of State, and, through it, to the President, that it was in the interests of the United States to support the elected government of South Vietnam, if South Vietnam was to survive.

Despite the importance the United States assigned to South Vietnam's independence, I developed the impression that Washington had too many theories for Vietnam and too little knowledge of it. I too had had no previous knowledge of the country, but the longer I stayed there, the more I felt that one had to get to know Vietnam, to live in it and to experience it, before one could recommend remedies. We Americans have a tendency to declare, "This is the way to do things." Then, six months later, we realize that we should have learned a lot more about a locality or a situation before we ventured to produce the answers. President Diem and his officials used to caution us on this score, and they were quite right. Of course, one can overdo it and have a paralysis of inaction in a situation requiring vigorous action.

As Ambassador, I tried to strike a balance between these two extremes. Our mission needed to show our own government the complexities of the situation in Vietnam, so that the administration would see that instant cures were not in the cards. At the same time, we needed prompt decisions and actions from Washington when required. Most important, we needed to encourage and stimulate effective measures on the part of the South Vietnamese government to engender loyalty and support in a war-weary people.

To accomplish these aims, we needed more than exhortations and public communiqués. We needed an agreed-upon plan and joint-action programs. Our relations with Washington were good. Our Country Team in Saigon functioned well. Our relations with the GVN improved markedly as confidence grew. The summer and fall of 1961 were spent laying the foundations for new programs, based on a new relationship with the GVN. This proved to be a sensitive, time-consuming task. Meanwhile, of course, the existing programs of American aid, some of long standing, continued.

4

Negotiating the U.S. Role in Vietnam

The struggle between Ngo Dinh Diem and Ho Chi Minh was essentially that of two nationalists, one a believer in individual self-determination, the other in communist regimentation, each trying to gain the people's support. Growing up on opposite sides of the Perfume River near Hue, Ho Chi Minh and Ngo Dinh Diem knew each other as young men, although Ho was older than Diem. Diem talked to me quite often about his rival, whose methods and philosophy he detested, but whose dedication to Vietnamese independence he respected. Thus Diem saw himself in a contest with Ho Chi Minh as to which nationalist leader the Vietnamese people were going to follow.

Winning the people of South Vietnam involved security, education, health, food, economic improvement, and justice, which together would build the basis for a more democratic system. These goals seemed obtainable in South Vietnam, but only under conditions of relative stability. With Viet Cong insurgency, intimidation, and destruction on the increase in many parts of the country, an effective military shield was a prime necessity. Urgently, we set about devising new programs of action with the government of South Vietnam, a task which consumed most of the summer and fall of 1961 and became, in fact, a continuing process.

Some background to these negotiations seems necessary. When I arrived in Vietnam, President Diem had a number of complaints against the U.S. government. Some were relatively trivial, such as our alleged failure to provide bulldozers in a timely manner, resulting in an inability to build local roads and airstrips on schedule. By far the most important were his charges of American interference in Vietnamese internal affairs. He did not want South Vietnam's responsibilities taken over by the United States. He did not want American forces to fight the battle for South Vietnamese independence and self-determination. "If we cannot win this struggle ourselves," he told me, "with the invaluable help you are giving, then we deserve to lose, and will lose." He was adamant about this because he felt that if the government of South Vietnam became dependent on the United States, it would merely prove the Viet Cong argument that "if you bow down to the United States, then you're going to find yourself an American colony, just as seventy-five years ago Vietnam became a French colony." On this sensitive point I was able to reassure him, since the whole idea behind the Task Force recommendations and my instructions from President Kennedy was that we were going to help the South Vietnamese maintain their freedom themselves, for themselves.

On many trips with President Diem in the country and in discussions with him and his ministers in Saigon, we developed an understanding essential to a successful joint undertaking. I felt that the cornerstone of mutual trust between our two countries had been laid. There remained the difficult task of devising effective joint programs of action. In this, we received valuable help from Washington.

In June 1961, a group of U.S. government officials, headed by Eugene Staley, President of the Stanford University Research Institute, was sent to Saigon to examine the Vietnamese economic situation and the thorny question of who was going to pay for increases in the size of the Vietnamese armed forces. The Staley group stayed for about a month, working closely with Arthur Gardiner, chief of our ICA (International Cooperation Agency) mission, General McGarr, and other military and economic officers of our mission. I found Staley sound and diplomatic in his approach and persuasive vis-à-vis the Vietnamese government, particularly President Diem, who continued to refer to Staley and his advice throughout my tenure in Saigon. Both the U.S. and Vietnamese governments endorsed the Staley mission's report, which dealt mainly with the financing of the GVN armed forces. (See the Appendix to this chapter for the text of the State Department's instructions to the Embassy, dated August 4, 1961, and President Kennedy's letter to Diem following the Staley visit, dated August 5, 1961.)

The Staley group was just one of many to visit South Vietnam. As time went on, the number of American visitors increased. Sometimes, as with Vice President Johnson's trip, we received high-level, high-profile visitors, sent expressly by the President or other top policymakers to examine the situation. At other times, our visitors were military or diplomatic officials en route to their posts, who stopped in as a courtesy, or through curiosity, to see how things were going. Often there were visits by members of Congress, who generally fell into one of two categories. Some Congressmen came to Saigon on nothing more than junkets. They arrived in groups, usually including their wives. As soon as they got off the plane, they would request the $500 in piastres they were entitled to draw from our aid program's counterpart funds and would then disappear into town. When they returned, they and the members of their party would be loaded down with china elephants and the like. Some of their planes must have been dangerously heavy when they left

Saigon, because those people took out a lot of loot. Other Representatives and Senators had more serious purposes for visiting Vietnam. With them we had thorough briefings and discussions, sharing each other's views and trying to figure out how to do things better. Another group of visitors comprised working-level officers or consultants sent to Saigon to look at specific situations or programs. The Staley mission fell into that category.

The most important and decisive survey mission we received in 1961 was the Taylor-Rostow mission. President Kennedy sent his military advisor, General Maxwell D. Taylor, and his Deputy Assistant for National Security Affairs, Walt W. Rostow, to Vietnam for an extensive survey. This was the first of many visits by the President's trusted advisors during my term. We learned rather suddenly of the Taylor-Rostow mission's arrival on October 18, but the news was welcome in Saigon. Although the Embassy and all its branches reported daily to the States and received daily guidance, we realized that Washington liked to send out people who had just been to a National Security Council meeting and who could report directly to the President upon their return. Such visits reflected the Kennedy style. They also gave the Embassy a chance to stay in close touch with policymakers in Washington.

The President had instructed General Taylor and Walt Rostow to make an extensive survey of the situation in Vietnam—economic, social, and political as well as military—and to report directly to him on their findings and recommendations. Accompanied by a large interagency group, they arrived fired with the desire to find ways to carry out more vigorously the programs agreed to with the Vietnamese government and to devise new ones.

The Taylor-Rostow mission went into all aspects of the situation. They traveled around Vietnam and held conferences with President Diem and members of his government, in which members of our Saigon mission participated. On the military side, Generals Lionel McGarr and Charles Timmes gave them the benefit of their military service and experience at the MAAG. Similarly, Arthur Gardiner contributed his knowledge and experience of the country's economic situation. Of particular importance was the problem of how to improve Vietnamese intelligence collection and reporting, and here the CIA staff, under Bill Colby's able leadership, helped devise better methods of intelligence collection, analysis, and coordination between the GVN and the United States. These and many other aspects of the total problem were studied in depth.

An unfortunate incident involving General McGarr occurred on October 24, the date of the Taylor-Rostow mission's second meeting with President Diem. Taylor and Rostow stayed in our home during their visit, and General McGarr joined us there before the meeting. When the cars arrived to take us to the meeting with Diem, Taylor turned to McGarr, saying, "General, we won't be needing you today." An expression of incredulity and hurt appeared on General McGarr's face. He just stood there while the rest of us drove off. Clearly, the decision had been made to transfer McGarr. I had had no idea that he was being recalled, and, to my knowledge, no one had notified him either.

Despite this disconcerting occurrence, the Taylor-Rostow mission had an important and fruitful visit, developing recommendations of far-reaching significance. Their report emphasized measures to build an *infrastructure* of democratic institutions—schools, communications, land usage, agriculture, economic development, and health facilities—behind a strengthened screen of physical security for the people. They helped work out in detail the programs for increased American assistance to South Vietnam which Kennedy had promised. The hope and expectation was that as these measures succeeded, the democratic concepts already written into the Vietnamese constitution would take hold and become more meaningful. Overall, I agreed with their report, feeling that it reinforced our instructions and what the mission was already trying to accomplish. Like Vice President Johnson's visit, the Taylor-Rostow mission put a seal of approval on the Kennedy administration's earlier decision to do more to support the South Vietnamese people's struggle through their elected government.

One item of the Taylor-Rostow report with which I did not agree was the recommendation to introduce a contingent of U.S. combat engineers into the Mekong Delta. The area had been badly flooded, and the report envisioned sending American combat engineers under the cover of flood relief. This would be a self-contained unit of about 5,000 men, able to defend itself in combat if cut off from South Vietnamese military support. Taylor and Rostow had added this idea during a layover in Baguio, where they actually wrote their report to the President, after their departure from Saigon. When I cabled my comments to Washington, I noted that I was in thorough accord with the ideas that had been discussed in Vietnam, but not with this new addition. My opposition stemmed from the conviction that the introduction of American combat forces would set a precedent and eventually lead to a shuffling of responsibility from the Vietnamese Army onto the stronger, better equipped Americans.

Pressures for a quick military solution were not uncommon in Washington. They reminded me of a story about the country doctor who used to give all of his patients, no matter what disease they had, a dose designed to throw them into "fits" because, he said, he was "hell on fits." In Vietnam there were many things that needed curing. I felt that it was better to treat each problem as best we could rather than send in American combat troops because we knew how to fight wars—of a different type.

I also opposed the idea because I felt that the cover was thin. The Mekong River floods the Delta practically every year. Although severe, the flood of 1961 really was nothing unusual. To bring in American combat forces covertly and contrary to the 1954 Geneva Accords seemed to invite an international issue, just at the time when the International Control Commission was condemning North Vietnam for its violations.[5] President Kennedy approved the Taylor-Rostow report and recommendations with the exception of the combat engineer unit, which he rejected. He drew a distinct line between U.S. military advisors and combat forces.

Retribution by South Vietnam against North Vietnam for its support of insurgency in the South was carefully considered at that time. There were some ongoing operations, sponsored by the CIA and carried out by South Vietnamese volunteers, to sabotage North Vietnamese installations being used against the South. Most of these attempts, however, had been unsuccessful or too costly and were being discontinued. Security in North Vietnam was very effective, particularly of its military-support installations.

At about this time, the idea of bringing in the British counterinsurgency expert Sir Robert G. K. Thompson arose. Thompson had been the British Permanent Secretary of Defense in Malaya and had had great success in helping the Malayans defend themselves, during a ten-year period in the 1950s, against the insurgents there, most of whom were Chinese in origin. I welcomed the British initiative. The Malayan experience was something of a counterpart to Vietnam, and we could learn from it. I felt this even more strongly after the British Advisory Mission, Vietnam, was established and we began working with Bob Thompson. Although Thompson consulted with Harry Hohler, the British Ambassador in Saigon, and probably used British Embassy communications to report back to Britain, he worked very closely with our mission. The British Foreign Office was not keen to get involved in the nitty-gritty of counterinsurgency in South Vietnam, so Thompson and his people worked rather independently as advisors.

Thompson had only about half a dozen people working for him, all of whom, I think, had served under Sir Gerald Templar in Malaya. They did not have much more than their individual experience to work with, but they were effective. They worked closely with the South Vietnamese and with us, advising on pacification and anti-infiltration methods. Thompson himself was very persuasive and had considerable influence with President Diem. We would sometimes go together to present a proposal to President Diem, who could see that Thompson knew what he was talking about and trusted him. In this he may have been influenced by the Tunku (President of Malaya), a close friend of President Diem, who spoke highly of Bob Thompson. I recall having dinner with President Diem and the Tunku, where the three of us discussed the similarities and dissimilarities of the insurgencies in Malaya and Vietnam. The Malayan President said, "If you fail here, we will have to start all over again in Malaya." He also reminded us that it took ten years for the British and Malayan forces to subdue the insurgency in his country.

The summer of 1961 saw the establishment in Saigon of a Joint Weapons Development Center, which came up with the idea, among others, of defoliation by the use of chemicals. The question of whether or not to use chemical defoliation was examined during the Taylor-Rostow mission, developing into a debate that lasted into the new year. I was dubious about the idea. Was it a necessary defense for the Vietnamese forces and their American advisors, and where would it lead? Vegetation grew thickly by the roads, the smaller roads especially, and provided excellent cover for Viet Cong ambushes. The South Vietnamese government felt that defoliation was necessary not only for defense against ambushes but also to deprive the Viet Cong of the rice and manioc on which they subsisted. The government thought that a program of spraying certain upland areas controlled by the Viet Cong would diminish the Viet Cong strength.

A conservationist friend, Harold Coolidge, visited us during these debates and was shocked by these plans, saying that the effects would spread and cause all kinds of damage. Although I did not see as far ahead as he did, I agreed with him, not only because defoliation (by spraying from airplanes) would destroy the beauty and disrupt the ecology of the countryside, but also because it could not be pinpointed. If the spray got into friendly villagers' gardens and rice paddies, it would kill those plants too. The same thing would happen if the chemicals got into their fish ponds. This would be in direct opposition to our efforts to build up Vietnam's agricultural economy. The key question was how accurately the spraying could be done. In the end, both governments agreed on a limited experiment, under strict guidelines. It was not very effective. The vegetation along the roads (mostly bamboo) grew back within two weeks after the spraying, as I saw from several observation flights. The plan was not extended, I think, until after American combat forces were deployed in 1965. Nevertheless, this was the beginning of a program which now, many years later, we can only deplore because of its hidden long-range dangers to health.

U.S.-Vietnamese cooperative arrangements had begun to take effect in 1961, reinvigorating and strengthening the relations which had existed since 1954 between the two countries and injecting a new note of confidence and hope. Pressing to infuse action into the programs we had agreed on, we were fortunate to have in Saigon an outstandingly able member of the Vietnamese government with whom to work. This was Nguyen Dinh Thuan, Secretary of the Presidency and later Coordinator of National Security, in effect President

Diem's civilian Chief of Staff. Though only in his thirties, Thuan had earned Diem's confidence and, despite some jealousies, the respect of his cabinet colleagues. He had the rare ability to make decisions, to get them approved, and to follow through on their implementation. He also had a saving sense of humor, however long he worked and however many his frustrations. I am happy to say that we continue our friendship to this day—he having escaped with a price on his head after the revolution that killed his President.

President Diem's office was at that time a small upstairs room in what used to be the residence of the French Governor General. While easily the most imposing looking building in Saigon—and hence called "the Palace"—its physical comforts were by no means palatial. Diem's office was extremely hot and ill-ventilated. A visit to the President could never be accomplished in less than an hour and generally required two or more. Hence it was a relief that, after the main features of the new agreements had been reached, we could deal with Nguyen Thuan to fit together the various pieces of our joint programs. Thuan's office was on the ground floor of "the Palace," and cooler than Diem's.

Our discussions and negotiations there were long and arduous enough, but Thuan was eager to move ahead, and he was easy and pleasant to deal with. He did, however, feel obliged to check out every important point with President Diem. This he generally did by going upstairs and returning promptly with Diem's agreement or a reasonable counterproposal, involving in the main a much closer American knowledge of the Vietnamese government's activities and the means to influence those actions supported by our aid. The overall concept was "pacification," a word expressing precisely our objective.

There were three principles underlying the new programs of increased U.S. aid to South Vietnam. One, the South Vietnamese, through their elected government, undertook to prosecute their struggle against the Viet Cong more intensively in all respects—economic, social, and political—behind a strengthened Vietnamese military shield. Two, the United States undertook to help by increased material aid and by advice and training. The introduction of U.S. combat forces was ruled out. President Diem did not want them, and President Kennedy did not want to send them. Three, there would be no interference by the United States in South Vietnam's internal affairs—no attempt to usurp the powers of the South Vietnamese government or to take control of the conduct of the struggle. Both parties agreed that pacification of the country had to be achieved by the Vietnamese themselves if it was to endure.

These principles formed the basis of a partnership of good faith directed toward a common end, the defense of the right of the South Vietnamese people to determine their own future without coercion, force, or terror. They rested on the premise that indigenous nationalism has to be the mainspring of resistance to communism, an idea I believe still holds true today. Finally, we had put together a program of action which seemed reasonably complete and promising. In particular, from my point of view, it fulfilled the American requirement to know in detail what was going on in each major field of activity—political, economic, social, and military—and provided a means to have our advice injected into these fields of action.

Quite unexpectedly one morning during these negotiations, Thuan returned from the President's office with a very disturbing question. President Diem, he said, was fully aware of the American insistence on knowing what was going on in the Vietnamese government on a continuing basis. He understood that this was a necessary condition for our increased aid and advice. But he was troubled. Who would be responsible for running the show? Who would have the ultimate authority—the Vietnamese government or the United States? More specifically, would the U.S. government, after providing aid and advice through the joint arrangements proposed, assume the right to insist upon having its way in the internal affairs and decisions of Vietnam?

This unexpected question sent me upstairs with Thuan to probe again President Diem's thoughts and hesitations. I found him in a suspicious mood. Things had been going badly in several provinces, he said. He was again being attacked in the American press. He was not of a mind—then or ever—to surrender the responsibility and authority to govern South Vietnam, so long as he held office under the constitution. Was the United States challenging this fundamental duty of his? Would we, in a pinch, use the leverage of our aid to threaten or destroy his government in case of disagreement?

I told him quite frankly that this question had not occurred to me before he raised it. I now understand his concern—and I considered it totally unfounded. There had been no hint of any such idea in discussions I had had with any American official, from President Kennedy and Vice President Johnson on down. We considered that we were dealing with a sovereign government, and my instructions made that clear. Furthermore, I strongly believed that advice from a friendly government, however persistent, was one thing; dictation or usurpation of authority was quite a different thing, and unacceptable. I agreed with him that even the appearance of U.S. control of GVN policy would weaken his government in its struggle for the loyalty of the Vietnamese people and would play into the hands of the Viet Cong. I knew that my government shared that view. We intended to use our new relationship to help the Vietnamese people through their constitutional government, not to make the final decisions for that government, and certainly not to undermine it. We did, however, insist upon having our views considered seriously by him and his government.

Finally, Diem asked me politely but pointedly to have what I had said to him confirmed by my government in Washington. Several days later, a cable from Washington arrived. Signed by Rusk and with the notation "from highest authority," meaning the President, it confirmed what I had told Diem. It was in effect a pledge that the U.S. government would work with him, not against him, so long as he remained the elected, constitutional President. Diem found this confirmation satisfactory.

Our joint undertakings were then launched in good faith. They provided vigorous new programs of action to protect the Vietnamese people and to win them solidly to the government's side—without enlarging the area of conflict, without inviting outside interference, without undercutting the essential spirit of Vietnamese nationalism, and without the use of American combat forces. The programs, later to be expanded, covered a wide range of activities. Examples included more schools and faster teacher-training; the use of hybrid seeds and imported fertilizers; better public relations and more "openness" in government; police training and the equipment of the Civil Guard; more systematic gathering and use of intelligence information on Viet Cong plans, acts, and movements, including infiltration from North Vietnam. To make the arrangement work in practice, it was necessary to establish a high degree of mutual confidence between the members of our mission in Saigon and the members of the Vietnamese government.

The new programs of action with the South Vietnamese government were now in place, but fundamental differences in pace and method remained. On the one hand, we had to cope, as well as we could, with the impatience that is so much a part of the American character and that especially typified the Kennedy administration. It is this quality that makes us chafe at building slowly and prudently, that makes us want to jump in, take over, and get the job done, even if in the long run it would be better to proceed at a slower pace. To do my job effectively, I would have to convey the complexity of the situation in Vietnam to the highest levels in Washington, so that they would judge progress in Vietnam according to standards appropriate for an undeveloped Asian country unaccustomed to democracy. On the other hand, we had to find a way to infuse a sense of urgency and direction into our Vietnamese partners, not only at the top, but throughout the government bureaucracy—and to do so without offending them. The key to this, we thought, was not necessarily more democracy, but greater efficiency and more follow-through. This, of course, involved persuading President Diem to relax his tight hold on the reins of government and to broaden its base. I felt that we could accomplish this in due time.

In retrospect, I failed to take fully into account the difference in perspective that exists between those in the field and their bosses in Washington. At the time, the incident with General McGarr was merely puzzling and discon-

certing. It did, however, indicate uneasiness or dissatisfaction in Washington
with the way things were going in Vietnam, a dissatisfaction that had not been
indicated to us in Saigon, and was not, in fact, articulated then. Hindsight
might even suggest that it presaged how Washington would deal with those
responsible for carrying out policy which it questioned but never explicitly
changed.

An interesting sidelight on how the Kennedy administration functioned
was revealed during this period. As a regular member of the Foreign Service,
I was not well known to most new members of the Kennedy administration,
nor was I particularly partisan in the political sense. I was not among the
"in" crowd at the White House.

Kenneth Galbraith, a close friend and confidant of the President, arrived
unexpectedly in Saigon while I was in the midst of the negotiations with the
Diem government described above. Ambassador Galbraith was on his way
from Washington to his post in New Delhi and had come via Saigon at the
President's request, apparently to check up on how we were doing. He stayed
at our home and was a stimulating houseguest, sending us afterward a number
of books, including many of his own.

The negotiations we were carrying on with President Diem and Minister
Thuan were extremely time-consuming, as were most things in Vietnam.
They involved delving into sensitive areas—the use of and accountability
for American counterpart funds, the broadening of Diem's government,
the role of the National Assembly, the concentration of power in the
hands of the President, the actual role of his brothers in the power structure. The treatment of Viet Cong prisoners and defectors and of those arrested or detained for "political crimes," the treatment of the Mont-
agnards, the alleged interference by President Diem in the operations of
his military commanders, his alleged favoritism in appointments, and a
number of other sensitive subjects were also fully discussed. To fulfill our
instructions (and my own imperatives), it was necessary to reach clarifica-
tions and understandings on these matters before agreeing specifically on
the use of American aid. At the same time, we had to do this discreetly
and privately, not as representatives of a powerful nation laying down the
law to its ally.

Galbraith was sent, no doubt, by President Kennedy to see whether I was
firm and persistent enough in these negotiations, but the slow tempo soon
got him down, and he departed for New Delhi while the talks were still in
progress. Some time later, John Richardson, who replaced Bill Colby as CIA
Station Chief in April 1962, told me of a surprising message he received from
New Delhi. Galbraith had asked his CIA man to get a private report from
Richardson on the conduct and outcome of the negotiations. "What did you

tell him, John?" I asked. "Highly satisfactory," he replied, "in outcome and in touch, although the press doesn't know it." Richardson knew that if the press had known about and publicized these tough negotiations, our influence with Diem would have been severely prejudiced, and the Viet Cong would have had a propaganda bonanza.

From this small incident, I began to suspect that President Kennedy relied more on news stories and reports from his cronies than he did on our cables, which were normally sent through the Department of State. Later on, when the Indian government seized the Portuguese enclave of Goa against the warnings of the United States, I was tempted to ask Richardson to enquire of his CIA colleague in New Delhi how effective Ambassador Galbraith's representations to the Indian government had been, but I refrained, considering it not to be my business.

A joint communiqué of January 4, 1962, announced an agreed program of action with the Republic of Vietnam. It spelled out the aims and undertakings of both governments: greater efforts on the part of the Republic of Vietnam to put down the insurgency, to pacify the country, to bring about democracy, to develop individual freedom and justice, and to improve the economic conditions of the people of South Vietnam. The United States, for its part, agreed to support these efforts by increasing its aid, materially, morally, and through increased advice and training. Specifically, the government of South Vietnam agreed to a partnership in this intensified effort, while retaining its sovereign rights as an independent government.

As this program gained momentum and began to reverse the tide of Communist success of the previous year, it was our aim that these improvements should be attributed to the Vietnam government. Often our mission played a decisive role, but despite the prodding of the American press, we chose not to boast about it or to emphasize our role. By giving the impression that the United States was twisting the arm of a government which was itself struggling to bring about improvements, we would only play into the Viet Cong's hands. Diem's government had to preserve, as a necessary element against the incessant Communist propaganda, its own individual, nationalist identity. It could not afford to become submerged by the colossus of the United States, coming in as its helper, advisor, and supporter. This was a cardinal point that the American press (and the top echelons of the Kennedy administration) never fully recognized.

APPENDIX

Telegram from the Department of State to the Embassy in Vietnam

Washington, August 4, 1961—7:41 p.m.

140. Task Force VN 22. This telegram constitutes the President's instructions for Ambassador Nolting and Task Force Saigon.

The following letter from President Kennedy to President Diem incorporates Task Force Saigon's suggestions in Embtel 145.

Ambassador Nolting is requested to transmit the letter to President Diem at once.

[Here follows the text of the letter from President Kennedy to President Diem, which Nolting delivered to Diem on August 6, *infra*.]

An essential part of Ambassador Nolting's presentation of the President's letter should refer to planning. In order to derive long-range benefits from our joint efforts to win in the present emergency, Viet-Nam needs long-range planning. To develop and carry out a long-range plan, Viet-Nam needs its own planners and the help of experts from outside. In the context of a long-range plan and considering the limitations that the agreed criteria place upon imports, the capital goods component of the commodity aid program can be expanded. It should be made clear that long-range planning and the increase in capacity to absorb capital goods will facilitate the flow of American development assistance. In focusing on such a Plan as an urgent item of current business, the nation can be inspired and consolidated. The U.S. is willing to help the long-range development effort with men and resources, and without diminishing in any way the U.S. support for the present counter-insurgency effort. We hope that one consequence of our new joint efforts will be an effective projection to the nation, its friends and its enemies, of our confidence in a long-range future for an independent Viet-Nam. In this connection, the Ambassador should seek discreetly to impress upon President Diem that he should use the total U.S. program for the greatest political effect in his achievement of maximum appreciation of his government by the people of Viet-Nam and the people of the world. (It is hoped that the Ambassador will continue his efforts to persuade President Diem to engage more fully in his civic action program re non-Communist elements now in political opposition.) This is, of course, part of a continuing effort that must be made with President Diem and his government generally.

Ambassador Nolting should make clear in his presentation that, if this is to be a truly joint effective effort, action by each country must be related to that by the other. In particular we attach great importance to the reasonable implementation of the agreed criteria governing imports; we also consider the raising of the effective piaster rate applicable to U.S. commodity aid, to which it is understood President Diem has already agreed, an indispensable part of our effort. Action by the GVN on both of

Source: Department of State, Central Files, 751K.5-MSP/7–3161. Secret: Priority. Drafted by Wood, Silver, and other members of the Vietnam Task Force; cleared with various other officers in the Departments of State, Defense, and the Treasury, as well as with the Bureau of the Budget, the International Cooperation Administration, and the President (per Rostow); repeated to CINC-PAC for PolAd; and pouched to Phnom Pehn, Bangkok, Vientiane, Paris, London, Ottawa, New Delhi, and Tokyo.

these matters will be very closely related to the U.S. contribution to the overall effort. The Ambassador may assure President Diem that increased piaster realization per dollar's worth of imports will not be used as a reason for reducing the American share of our joint efforts.

President Diem and his government need to be reminded of adverse criticism that our Viet-Nam program has experienced in the Congress and in the American press generally favorable to his cause, and to be discreetly warned that the program cannot profit from further attack. In the avoidance of such attack, the GVN itself plays the essential role.

Ball

Letter from President Kennedy to President Diem

Washington, August 5, 1961.

DEAR MR. PRESIDENT: Dr. Eugene Staley has told me personally of the mission which he and his special financial group undertook to Viet-Nam at my request. He has told me of the courteous and understanding welcome he received from you and from the members of your government, and has described to me the progress you have already made despite the great difficulties of Communist subversion which you face. I was pleased to hear of the cooperative and friendly spirit which animated the meetings of the Vietnamese and American experts. It is particularly encouraging to me that this spirit of cooperation, which was embodied in the joint undertakings of the counter-insurgency plan and which was so evident during the visit of Vice President Johnson, will now be carried on through the very practical medium of parallel Vietnamese and American committees.

I have examined the joint action program which the Vietnamese and American experts propose and I heartily agree with the three basic tenets on which their recommendations are based, namely:

1. Security requirements must, for the present, be given first priority.

2. Military operations will not achieve lasting results unless economic and social programs are continued and accelerated.

3. It is in our joint interest to accelerate measures to achieve a self-sustaining economy and a free and peaceful society in Viet-Nam.

I also agree that we are more likely to succeed if both of our countries take adequate action now than if we react to the Communist threat by slow and insufficient measures.

I consider that the joint action program put before us by our expert groups offers a sound foundation on which our two governments can build rapidly and successfully. Therefore, having in mind your letter of June 9 and the strong recomendation of Ambassador Nolting, I should like to inform you that the United States will provide equipment and assistance in training as needed for an increase in the armed forces of Viet-Nam from 170,000 to 200,000 men. In order to make such an increase as effective as possible I suggest that before the time when the level of 170,000 is reached

Source: Washington National Records Center, RG 84, Saigon Embassy Files; FRC 66 A 878, 350 GVN-TF-SFG. Attached to the source text is a copy of the letter of transmittal, dated August 6, from Nolting to Diem.

our governments should satisfy themselves on the following points: (1) That there then exists a mutually agreed upon, geographically phased strategic plan for bringing Viet-Cong subversion in the Republic of Viet-Nam under control; (2) That on the basis of such a plan there exists an understanding on the training and use of these 30,000 additional men; (3) That the rate of increase from 170,000 to 200,000 will be regulated to permit the most efficient absorption and utilization of additional personnel and material in the Vietnamese armed forces with due regard to Viet-Nam's resources.

I also suggest, in view of the fact that the force level of 200,000 will probably not be reached until late in 1962, that decision regarding a further increase above 200,000 be postponed until next year when the question can be re-examined on the basis of the situation which we shall then be facing. Meanwhile, the buildup in equipment and training of the Civil Guard and Self Defense Corps within already agreed levels should be expedited.

Returning to the joint action program, I am most encouraged to learn of the large measure of agreement reached by our expert groups on the steps required to meet the piaster financing problems posed by the joint action program. It seems to me that in the light of these recommendations we can move forward simultaneously on measures to solve this problem by a combination of actions by the two governments: by the Government of the United States, within the limits of available funds, to provide the external resources which are required, including commodity imports which can be justified and absorbed under the seven criteria of the joint action program; and by the Government of Viet-Nam, to generate the piasters to direct the resources of Viet-Nam to the highest priority requirements. The several means to acquire such piasters are spelled out in the joint action program. I hope that our parallel committees can immediately cooperate in working out target estimates for an import program which will give both our governments a basis for planning.

The early implementation of the joint recommendation of the expert groups regarding tax reform and the principle of a single and realistic rate of exchange, using methods which take into account the political and psychological factors which I know you have to weigh, will certainly increase the effectiveness of American aid to Viet-Nam. I hope this recommendation can be implemented soon. Within the limits of funds to be made available by the Congress and within the agreed criteria, my policy shall be to help you as much as possible to achieve a break-through in your efforts to bring security to your people and to build toward economic independence.

Turning to the experts' joint recommendations for emergency social action and to the direct aid programs already under way, I am asking Mr. Labouisse, Director of International Cooperation, to conduct through USOM Viet-Nam a thorough and expeditious review with your experts of the new proposals and of other programs which these proposals were intended to supplement. Among these I mention as of special interest the fields of communications, including television and radio; agrovilles, land development, agricultural credit and agricultural extension; extended assistance to road building; continued efforts to expand education, particularly primary and elementary education in the villages; training for rural administration; and plans to assure more and better equipped and trained officials, adequately compensated, especially in rural areas and in the villages. Our basic premise is that these programs be designed with your government to meet your needs and conditions, and that they be carried out by your people, with our assistance where required. I especially wish USOM to offer whatever help you think will be most effective to strengthen the vital ties of loyalty between the people of Free Viet-Nam and their government.

As an integral part of our efforts to meet the current crises, I believe it is essential that we continue and expand the progress which has already been made toward the long range development of Viet-Nam. The emergency measures which we undertake should be solidly anchored—as soon as possible—in a comprehensive long range planning process to determine the best uses which can be made of available resources on a time-phased basis. Only in this way can we adequately meet the long and short term requirements which interact in the problems which our two countries must solve together. This will require the creation of more effective planning machinery as recommended in the joint report of our experts. In addition to development of a long range plan, the training of staff to carry on planning activities (covering such matters as the use of medical manpower and teachers for which Viet-Nam has competing civilian-military requirements) might be expedited. I urge that our parallel committees develop specific projects in line with the general recommendations of the report.

In the face of competing and urgent demands for aid and assistance from countries throughout the world we shall make our contribution to the future of Viet-Nam. Our support of Viet-Nam's independence and development will, as I have assured you in the past, remain among the highest priorities of American foreign policy. As indicated above, we are prepared to commit, within the limits of our available aid funds, substantial resources to assist you in carrying out the military and economic and social components of the special action program. In order to speed the action during this emergency period and to permit greater flexibility I should like to emphasize that the chief responsibility for the planning and execution of the American share of the program will, more than ever, rest with Ambassador Nolting and, under his direction, with MAAG and USOM. In this connection I hope that, with the delegation of maximum authority to the parallel committees as recommended by our experts, the committees will assure follow-up action, approve modifications of the program and "recommend measures to improve and adapt the special action program as the situation changes."

In conclusion I believe that we have now agreed on sound ways to strengthen the Vietnamese economy and Vietnamese security in the face of the mounting Communist threat. Now we can proceed to develop additional concrete plans and carry them out rapidly and effectively.

I firmly believe that if our countries continue to work so effectively together, the Almighty will grant us the strength and the will to succeed.

With warm personal regards,
Sincerely,

John F. Kennedy

5

The Military Picture and Pacification

At dawn on the morning of February 27, 1962, my wife sat up in bed and said, "Bombs or close-in artillery!" "It's only a thunderstorm," I muttered, but quickly realized she was right.

The telephone rang. A Marine guard at the Embassy reported aircraft dropping bombs on the President's Palace. "Whose aircraft?" In the dim light and fog, the Marine first thought they were Chinese planes, then American, and finally he recognized their South Vietnam markings. The planes circled slowly at a low altitude over the Palace, dropping their bombs and strafing with 20mm guns. Antiaircraft fire soon opened up—from Vietnamese Navy craft in the Saigon River, as it turned out. After a short time of intense firing, the racket ceased.

Several members of our mission gathered in our bedroom, where emergency communications equipment was kept, but this was of little use in finding out exactly what had happened. I pulled on some clothes, got into our car, and directed the driver to the Palace. The car had a small American flag on the front fender, and this got us through the police cordon, but the Palace was surrounded by ARVN (Army of the Republic of South Vietnam) tanks. We could not drive through. I impulsively jumped out and walked toward the gates. A sharp bayonet prick in the back stopped me. I explained who I was and was let through the gates.

The building was smoldering, evidently badly damaged. Ngo Dinh Nhu was walking around outside in the gardener's pants. (He explained that he had borrowed them because his own had been destroyed in his bedroom.) He was greatly worried about his wife. Madame Nhu had fallen through the bedroom floor and had been taken to a hospital, badly lacerated but not seriously injured, as it turned out. Their infant daughter, alive and unhurt, had been found in the arms of her dead amah (nurse), who had been killed by a falling beam. The three other Nhu children also were not injured. I noticed several dead deer in the park.

President Diem soon joined Counselor Nhu and me on the grounds. He had just made a radio announcement, calling for calm and explaining what had happened. Before dawn, three pilots of the Vietnamese Air Force were dispatched on a mission to bomb a Viet Cong stronghold. Instead, they decided to bomb the President's Palace (which housed both living quarters and offices for President Diem and the Nhu family). From intercepts of radio messages between the pilots, which we later obtained, their main target was the wing occupied by the Nhu family. This was evident from the damage I saw that morning. One of the planes was shot down by the Navy's antiaircraft guns and fell into the Saigon River. Another escaped to Cambodia. I am not sure what happened to the third pilot. I think it was determined later that he was not involved in the actual bombing.

The attack was clearly the independent work of three dissident Air Force pilots. There was no evidence to link their actions to the Vietnam Air Force command—in fact, all evidence we got was to the contrary. The Army responded promptly by sending tanks to protect the Palace, and the Navy responded with its antiaircraft batteries. At that time, in contrast to the unsuccessful coup attempt in 1960 and the successful one in 1963, the armed forces of South Vietnam were loyal to their government. Calm quickly returned to Saigon. Our children left for school that morning as usual. My wife had walked to the Truehearts' house (my deputy, Bill Trueheart, and his wife were away) and brought their younger son to our house for safety.

A major development of early 1962 was the creation of a U.S. Military Assistance Command, Vietnam (MACV). We in Saigon had heard in late 1961 that Washington planned to separate the mission into two coequal parts with divided authority and responsibility. A four-star general would command the military side, while the rest would be under the Ambassador. MACV would have a more active role in Vietnamese military affairs and would incorporate the Military Assistance Advisory Group (MAAG) into its structure. MACV itself would be a subregional command, reporting to the Commander-in-Chief in the Pacific and responsible for U.S. military affairs in Thailand as well as Vietnam.

I had doubts about the wisdom of establishing MACV. Creating a subtheater command in Vietnam would bring the United States closer to a combat role than we had been previously, I felt, and certainly closer than was envisioned earlier under the Kennedy and Eisenhower administrations. Also, splitting the mission between the Ambassador and the MACV commander could have serious adverse consequences. On the working level, we customarily had joint meetings in my office with the military, State, AID, CIA, and USIA representatives. We seldom failed to agree. Under a split mission, the questions of who would chair such meetings, who would take the lead in forming a consensus, who would be in charge in a major crisis could cause trouble, creating unnecessary friction among the mission's various elements. On a higher plane, it was vital in an emergency that one person be in charge and that everyone in the mission know who that individual was. Finally, splitting the mission directly contradicted President Kennedy's instructions to me that Saigon was to be a *unified* mission. I was concerned that the United States speak with one voice to the government and people of South Vietnam.

I raised these issues with Secretary McNamara at the first Secretary of Defense conference on Vietnam, held in Honolulu in December 1961. At that time the various proposals for MACV were on the table in Washington. Although the conference did not address these questions formally, I discussed them in private conversations with McNamara. I suspect that the idea originated either with him, General Maxwell Taylor, or the Joint Chiefs of Staff. McNamara was courteous and friendly as always, but he was unresponsive to my arguments. Soon thereafter, we received in Saigon the directive creating MACV and naming General Paul Harkins its head. The directive, although somewhat vague on the subject, contained the idea of the split mission. It was circulated throughout the Pacific Command, from Korea and Japan to Australia and the Philippines.

The question of what this directive meant in terms of U.S. policy and of who was ultimately in charge of the U.S. mission in Saigon was important. I flew back to Washington in January 1962 to try to resolve it. I spoke first with Secretary of State Dean Rusk. He gave me little clarification, commenting, "It doesn't make any real difference." I said I thought it was a question of importance. It could make a great difference in the orientation of the mission, in whether its influence became more military and less political, economic, and social. It could make a critical difference in an emergency. When Rusk said, "Oh, forget it, Fritz. You can get along with Paul Harkins," I responded, "Dean, it's not a question of anticipating problems or being jealous of a prerogative, or anything of that sort. I am just trying to get my orders clear, and to see whether there's been any change in the thinking of my bosses in Washington, including the President." But Rusk did not want to get involved.

I received a similar reception from McNamara. He was cordial but essentially noncommittal on the subject. Finally, I spoke with Averell Harriman, who had replaced Walt McConaughy as Assistant Secretary of State for Far Eastern Affairs in December. Harriman took my point, saying, "Well, if we can't get any interest here, let's go and see the President about it." He arranged for us to meet with President Kennedy about the matter.

Only the President, Harriman, General Maxwell Taylor, and I were present at the White House meeting. Harriman explained the purpose of our call, and I added: "Mr. President, I hope you don't think I'm fool enough to try to run or intervene in military matters, training or logistics, or things of that sort, which I don't know much about. But the problem is that there can be

misunderstandings down the line, there can be emergencies in which some-
body has to come up with the U.S. position. I fear there will be trouble if
this is not clarified." The President immediately agreed. Stating that he wanted
a unified mission in Saigon, as his original directive had specified, he turned
to General Taylor and said, "Max, rewrite that directive and get this clear:
the Ambassador is in overall charge." Harriman and I had previously marked
up a copy of the directive to make it clear and satisfactory from our point of
view. The President glanced at our changes and told General Taylor again to
rewrite the directive. The President did not suggest or indicate any change
in policy.

Bob McNamara had business in Honolulu, and he graciously invited me
to fly that far with him on my return trip to Saigon. While we were eating
dinner on the plane, the subject of MACV and the split mission arose. I said,
"Bob, I hope you understand what this was all about." He said he did, but
that there was nothing he could do as Secretary of Defense, because the Joint
Chiefs of Staff were adamant that "no four-star general is going to be under
an Ambassador." The President would have to decide the issue. I told him
that the President had done so—as I thought he had. I repeated that I had
no intention of meddling in military matters and ending by saying, "If you
want to tie this can to your tail and make this into a real war, that's not my
decision, but I can't have the responsibility from the President and not have
the authority." McNamara said quite frankly, "Look, on this one the Joint
Chiefs have got me over a barrel. I can't do anything about it." And, as much
as I respect Max Taylor, I suspect that McNamara may have been speaking of
him as well. (General Taylor was still President Kennedy's military aide. He
would not become Chairman of the Joint Chiefs of Staff until July.)

A new directive about MACV was issued a couple of weeks later. Although
some language was changed, it was ambiguous and fuzzy. It still talked about
divided responsibilities and really did not clarify matters at all. This bothered
me, but I was less uneasy than before. I had met Paul Harkins while I was
in Honolulu, where he was serving under Admiral Felt as the Army's Deputy
to the Commander in Chief Pacific Area Command (CINCPAC). We had talked
in his office for about half a day. We had a meeting of minds, and I was
impressed by his understanding. After he came to Saigon, Paul Harkins and
I became close friends and worked well together. There were very few cases
where authority and responsibility became an issue, and these usually arose
farther down the line. When they got to us, we readily resolved them. General
Harkins' Chief of Staff, Lieutenant General Richard Weede (U.S. Marine Corps),
proved to be equally cooperative and effective in handling the internal relations within our mission and relations with the Vietnamese military. He too
was a real soldier-statesman. Under different circumstances, however, the

outcome could have been far less good. When members of our military establishment receive a new or enlarged assignment, they generally seize it with an overwhelming zeal. I was determined that our mission should not become predominantly military, because Vietnam's problems then were only partly military. Fortunately, MACV (and Admiral Felt at CINCPAC) saw it in much the same light.

President Diem shared my first reservations about MACV when I discussed its establishment with him. Contrary to much of what has been written about Diem, he did not want his country caught up in an intensified military undertaking. Rather, he viewed our joint program as a social, political, and economic effort to pacify the country, to be implemented behind a military shield of protection, and wondered why the United States was upgrading the MAAG to a subregional command. He was concerned that the struggle in Vietnam not become an international military affair, feeling that it should be a Vietnamese effort. He wanted to avoid attaching any stigma of colonialism to his government. Also, he feared that MACV's creation would be viewed as a violation of the Geneva Accords, provoking adverse reactions from the International Control Commission. In the end, however, Paul Harkins and the working relationship he developed with the rest of the mission and the South Vietnamese government mitigated Diem's unease as well as my own.

The Army of South Vietnam was in transition in early 1962. It had been less than a year since President Kennedy approved the Counterinsurgency Plan for Vietnam. Previous U.S. military efforts had aimed at preparing South Vietnam's defenses for a possible invasion from the North, as in Korea ten years before. The Army of the Republic of Vietnam (ARVN) had been built, trained, and equipped principally with this in mind. Under the influence of people like Ed Lansdale in Washington and Bob Thompson in Saigon, this emphasis shifted to the concept of fighting the Viet Cong by different means, that is, defeating subversion from within rather than invasion from without. Both the civilian and military elements of the American mission accepted this concept. But the actual conversion from conventional warfare to a counterinsurgency effort—going from a divisional structure to a battalion concept, changing the types of equipment, adjusting communications, and getting the South Vietnamese military to appreciate and accept these changes—took longer. Sometimes, I think, individual ARVN officers and old-time American advisors found it difficult to adjust to the change.

Clearly, the balance between civil and military matters occupied much of our time during my two and one-half years in Vietnam. But although we recognized their importance, both President Diem and I saw military measures as the means that would, if successful, allow us to do our real work: pressing on with the economic, political, and social aspects of our joint programs. Our goal was to create in South Vietnam a society capable of retaining its freedom and of sustaining a more democratic government. The first step, we agreed, was to pacify the countryside. As this was being accomplished, reforms would be introduced and sustained.

By far the most important effort in this area also became the most famous, the Strategic Hamlets program, initiated formally by the South Vietnamese government in February 1962. This initiative was a modification of the agroville program of the 1950s, in which peasants were moved to large fortified areas protected by the ARVN.[6] I visited several agrovilles which appeared staunch and stable, but the program to build them had been discontinued, reportedly because it forcibly uprooted people and moved them far from their ancestral homelands. President Diem never admitted it, but this criticism was probably valid, and most people thought the agrovilles were failures, at least in terms of popular support.

Based on this experience and Bob Thompson's work in Malaya, the Strategic Hamlets program was less ambitious in terms of size and displacement of people. The hamlets themselves were small. People were not required to move but were encouraged to fortify and defend themselves in the areas where they already lived, sometimes by regrouping their houses. As Thompson envisioned it, the hamlets would follow an "oil blot" pattern. First they would be established in relatively secure areas. When these hamlets became stable, more would be established on their outskirts. Their effect would thus spread outward from several central points, eventually intersecting so that most of the countryside would be defensible. The United States provided material aid, building materials, barbed wire, ammunition, and guns for the volunteer village militia, boosting the effort substantially.

When it was launched, the Strategic Hamlets program became Ngo Dinh Nhu's principal interest. In fact, Nhu, together with Thompson, sold the idea to President Diem. Counselor Nhu was more imaginative than his brother and, in some respects, less rigid in his thinking. Nhu supported the Strategic Hamlets program actively, did much to get it going, worked at it constantly, and talked about it incessantly. Practically the first words out of his mouth anytime I saw him were "Hameaux Stratégiques." I teased him about this once, which was probably a mistake. "Qu'est-ce que c'est, Monsieur le Conseiller? What are these Strategic Hamlets?" He looked at me absolutely dumbfounded. Finally, he realized it was a joke, although I suspect he did not find it amusing.

The Strategic Hamlets program and Nhu's administration of it (he headed the Interministerial Committee that oversaw it) have been panned unmercifully as a forced resettlement program that created resentment among the peasants. Some of that criticism may have been justified, although I saw no evidence to support it in the hamlets themselves. The charge that Nhu was trying to establish too many strategic hamlets too fast, instead of using the "oil blot" approach, probably had some merit. Sometimes we thought: "Maybe this thing is moving too fast. There aren't enough weapons for the small home guards to use. The ARVN is not positioned to defend some of these hamlets, which, if attacked, can't hold out more than a day." But to be fair, it was difficult, once the idea caught on, for the government to say no when the province chiefs recommended additional hamlets in their areas. (I concede that we could not determine to what extent the province chiefs were doing this to curry favor with the Diem regime. We could only judge the results.)

Another criticism by the media was that in order to impress the U.S. government and the Vietnamese people with the size and success of the program, Nhu admitted hamlets into it before they could in reality defend themselves. We could not dismiss this charge lightly, because some of the hamlets were attacked and overrun during or shortly after their construction. But clearly the Viet Cong and Hanoi were alarmed and set back by the Strategic Hamlets program and its rapid growth. We learned this from many intelligence sources—radio intercepts, captured Viet Cong, captured documents, "Chieu Hoi" (Open Arms) defectors, and others. The fortified hamlets cut off the Viet Cong's access to food supplies and manpower—or forced them to fight to obtain them.

It was also alleged in the press (and later by the U.S. government) that Nhu padded the figures relating to the strategic hamlets to make the program appear stronger than it was. In early 1963, I accompanied him on a trip to inspect some of the hamlets. At that time, there were about 15,000 hamlets officially classified as "strategic." The government had a list of everything that had to be done within a hamlet before it could be accepted into the program. On this particular day, we were going to see one that had just been designated a strategic hamlet. As we flew there, I asked Nhu, "Mr. Counselor, how many of these hamlets do you think are really solid, in the sense of being ready to fight if the Viet Cong attack in strength, and if the inhabitants don't know whether or not there's an ARVN battalion within ten miles to help them?" Nhu thought a while and said, "Right now, less than 30 percent are that good, but they're getting better, I think, and with further successes, that percentage will increase." I had expected him to say, "Oh, all of them."

The allegations that people were being uprooted as in the agroville program and forced to go miles to their fields and to leave their ancestors' burial places resurfaced with the Strategic Hamlets program. But I found this to be true only to a small extent. The hamlets were not large enough to bring people far from where they lived and farmed. Most house locations remained unchanged, with only a few brought in from the outskirts. My observation after seeing a number of hamlets was that the resettlement of the peasants was voluntary, without coercion on the part of the government.

On the whole, I thought that the strategic hamlet was a sound concept and that its results were good. Of course, criticism arises from any program, no matter how sound its design or how efficient its execution. It was better, we thought, to try this admittedly imperfect plan than to let the villages get overrun and looted by the Viet Cong with little or no resistance.

More people were glad to have the hamlets than the press indicated. It was impossible to take a true census, but of the many strategic hamlets I visited, I do not recall one that seemed to be a resettlement in which the people were forced to participate. I remember vividly visiting a hamlet that was just being constructed in a province in the Mekong Delta. One old man was bringing the poles from his house, which was across the stream, into the slightly fortified area. I asked him, "Don't you have anybody to help you to do this?" "No," he replied, pointing to the woods, "my sons are with the Viet Cong. But once we get our house here, where it is defensible, I'm sure they'll come back."

Other developments strengthened my conviction that the pacification efforts were working slowly but surely and that the attempts at social reform were taking hold. By the end of 1962, my family and I could drive to Cape St. Jacques or Dalat without armed escort. A year earlier, we would have certainly been ambushed. Large areas of the country had become stable. In 1962 and early 1963, for example, the schools in many provinces had so many students that they ran on staggered schedules, holding up to three sessions a day. Primary, intermediate, and secondary school teachers were being trained, and new vocational schools opened, encouraged and partly financed by the Agency for International Development. There students learned many skills, from agriculture to mechanics. Other U.S. AID programs helped to train administrators to work for the South Vietnamese government in the provinces. Over 2,000 of Vietnam's civil servants had been murdered by the Viet Cong in 1960, yet there were applications for the vacancies. The educational improvements represented vital advances for Vietnam, where skilled labor and professional workers were scarce. In the area of health improvements, the combined efforts of the U.S., Australian, Philippine, Canadian, Japanese, and South Vietnamese governments brought the incidence of malaria down from 7.6 percent in 1961 to less than 2 percent in 1963.

In 1962 and the first five months of 1963, I was confident that the Republic of Vietnam was gradually winning the battle against the Viet Cong insurgency. So were my colleagues of the diplomatic corps, representing eighteen countries which had recognized South Vietnam and sent ambassadors to Saigon.

Most of the members of our Country Team were optimistic. So was the administration in Washington. Ho Chi Minh was quoted by the Australian journalist Wilfred Burchett as conceding, "1962 was Diem's year." Were we mistaken or overconfident? I don't think so. What was required was patience and perseverance on the course we were pursuing.

Joe Mendenhall left the mission in the summer of 1962 still convinced that a military government was what Vietnam needed, and that Diem was not. I suspect that my friend Arthur Gardiner retained his doubts about the Diem regime when he transferred to Tokyo around the same time. But John Richardson, Joe Brent (Gardiner's replacement), Paul Harkins, and I all felt that our joint program was moving well. And I certainly received no indication from John Mecklin, of USIA, that he thought our Embassy was a "mission in torment," as he titled his book about his experiences there.

We worked hard and were constantly in touch with each other. The American mission had more than a thousand pairs of eyes and ears out in the provinces, in practically all areas of South Vietnam. These were the people with the Operations Mission, the military advisors, the Foreign Service language officers, members of the CIA, and our consular officers in Hue. Some spoke Vietnamese; all constantly observed and reported on the conditions in the provinces and on various facets of the pacification efforts throughout South Vietnam.

In addition to the work of these salaried employees, we had the volunteer work of the American wives, organized in the American Women's Association of Saigon (AWAS). Their activities included work in leprosaria, maternity clinics, occupational therapy centers for Vietnam veterans and other hospitals, orphanages, and schools for the blind; classes and conversation groups for Vietnamese women who wanted to learn or improve their English; and financial grants to students.

As a result of these volunteer efforts, the mortality rate at the Go Vap Orphanage outside Saigon dropped from 80 percent to 20 percent in one year; a community center, which served as a day nursery and kindergarten for children of working parents during the day and as an adult education center at night, was built in one of Saigon's poorest sections; a hospital where starving babies were nursed back to health and their families educated in health and nutrition was constructed; the Tribes Clinic at Dalat, where an American missionary nurse treated Montagnard illnesses and dispensed as much health education and welfare as possible, received assistance; and the babies of lepers, who are usually not infected with the disease but should be kept isolated for two years to be sure they are free from the contagion, got improved diets and living conditions, as well as much love and care. Contrary to the impression that has been given over the years, getting willing and able American help, both from employees and volunteers, was not a problem in Vietnam. Administering these activities tactfully, so that we helped the Vietnamese without challenging the incumbent authorities, was sometimes a problem, but one AWAS managed to surmount. It is noteworthy that Vietnamese Buddhists and Christians, Taoists and Confucians worked together with our wives, with no indication of religious friction.

Of course, there were ups and downs, good days and bad. Nothing ever seemed to work perfectly in Vietnam. In late May and June of 1962, Vietnam experienced a financial crisis when the government became concerned about a shortage of piastres. President Diem asked the United States for more imports of consumer goods and for a waiver of the "Buy American" rules, under which American funds could be used to buy only products made by American companies. These regulations did increase costs, although not significantly, and delayed the completion of some projects. Waivers were sometimes granted, so that South Vietnam was able to buy barbed wire for the Strategic Hamlets program from Australia, for example, but overall the "Buy American" rules were retained. I do not recall any severe setbacks or losses because of them.

Unfortunately, however, the economic improvements we hoped to achieve never fully materialized. The Vietnamese government did have a foreign exchange surplus in 1962 through its exports of rice and rubber, and U.S. imports generated counterpart funds from which the South Vietnamese armed forces were paid, but the economy was unable to stand entirely on its own. It was overburdened by the pressing needs of protection and defense. The Vietnamese government was still not efficient, but it was gradually improving. Administrators coming out of the AID schools were well motivated, but lacked experience, knowledge, and know-how in many cases. (So did we, for that matter.) Those who did accomplish things quickly became Viet Cong targets. This situation, I am confident, would have improved with more time, but in the end, we did not have it.

We also encountered the day-to-day difficulties that arise in any joint program of action. Through no fault of their own, people often see only those aspects of a problem with which they are directly concerned. When, for example, the price of pork was lowered by decree in Saigon, the U.S. Operations Mission (USOM) officer responsible for encouraging pig-raising throughout South Vietnam took it as a repudiation of his program. He immediately complained to the American journalists in Saigon, who used the story as an example of the lack of coordination within our mission and with the Vietnamese government. Actually, there were good reasons for the decree, which this officer understood and accepted when they were explained to him. I do not by any means contend that our multifaceted operations were perfectly coordinated, but I do contend that the media generally exaggerated the defects.

By far the gravest problem we faced was also the most overwhelming. We were trying to foster democracy in an Asian society that had had no experience with it until 1955. The institutions and infrastructure to support it simply were not present in South Vietnam in the early 1960s. They had to be developed, a slow, painstaking process under the best of circumstances. That this society was under attack from forces within and outside it, whose professed goal was to overthrow it, severely compounded the problem. Most of our mission, I think, realized this, and laid aside their frustrations in light of it.

One impediment to furthering democracy was that Vietnamese society was very cliquish. People who had attended better schools, or who had attained academic excellence, considered themselves superior to those who had gone to other schools or had ranked lower academically. This was true in both military and civilian circles. I had this fact pointed out to me graphically after I gave a speech before the Saigon Rotary Club on January 15, 1962.

I thought hard about that speech, trying to decide whether to make it bland, or to really say something. Saigon was very volatile, quite different politically from the countryside. Many critics of the Diem regime lived in the city. They were mainly from the elite upper class. Calling themselves "intellectuals," they wrote many letters to the newspapers denouncing the government. Though some of their criticisms were valid, I felt that these dissidents would have accomplished more if they had directed their energies toward working within the government to change things for the better. In the end, I decided to use the occasion to address this problem. I said, in effect, what a difference it would make in free Vietnam's survival if those who criticized and plotted against the government would join it and pull together against the common enemy, the Viet Cong. My words fell on deaf ears. The intellectuals continued to send their scathing letters, and quite a few prominent people were offended by my talk.[7]

A surprising effect the speech had was that President Diem called me and asked, "Have you got any ideas as to who might strengthen this government?" When I replied that I did, he said, "Well, please let me see the list." I returned to my office, made a list, and took it to him. He stated, "If you can persuade any of these people to serve, I would be delighted to have them in my government." I thought this was an unusual request—asking a foreign diplomat to talk to other Vietnamese who were dissident or hostile to the government—but, having already stuck my neck out, I agreed. Not one of the people I spoke with was willing to join the government. Several said that they would not serve under Ngo Dinh Diem because they were better educated than he was, or had stood higher in school. One man said that he would serve as Minister of the Interior, provided the President gave him full control over the police and promised never to interfere with his use of them. When I reported the results of my survey to President Diem, he said, "You see, that is my problem."

Another incident in 1962 demonstrated how thoroughly Western the concept of democracy is, how alien it was to the culture of Vietnam, and how deeply authoritarian rule was ingrained in the Vietnamese people. Several members of the National Assembly, the elected legislative body, came to my office to request my intervention with President Diem on a bill the Assembly has passed (the so-called Blue Laws). "How did you vote on this bill?" I inquired. "We voted in favor." "Why," I asked, "did you vote for it if you were against it?" "Because the government proposed it," they replied. "Yet now," I continued, "you are asking me, a foreign diplomat, to try to prevent its implementation?" "Yes, exactly. You see," they explained, "we did not feel it would be proper for us to oppose in Parliament a measure recommended by our president." "Why?" I asked. "Did you fear reprisals?" "Not from the government—it is only that we know our constituents would not understand it if we opposed a measure proposed by the government."

I took their request to President Diem, who deplored the fact that the Assembly had failed to exercise its independent responsibility. He sent the bill back to the Assembly for a second reading with modifications. It was again overwhelmingly approved, despite, I am sure, the real feelings of a majority of the members.

Because of experiences like these, when Washington instructed us to persuade Diem to broaden the base of his government and to introduce more democratic institutions and methods, we would try to get these instructions clarified. What did they mean by more democracy? How was it to be accomplished, and in what time span? Where did Washington want us to start, with village elections (which had already begun) or with a constitutional change in the methods of electing the National Assembly or the President? My point was that these vague instructions calling for more democracy were unachievable in the short run, not because of the character of the Diem government, but because the foundations for democracy as we know it had to be developed over a long period of time.

Diem himself was certainly not without faults. He remained unable or unwilling to delegate authority. He was suspicious of his subordinates, in particular his military officers. Additionally, while he himself placed no store in personal belongings or money, his sense of pride in his country motivated him to insist upon trappings he felt necessary and appropriate for a head of state. Thus, his public and official entertainments were sometimes more lavish than the condition of his country seemed to warrant. His enemies seized upon this to imply personal corruption. To my knowledge, such allegations were totally unjustified. Diem's personal quarters were small and austere, and he showed no interest whatsoever in acquiring wealth or property for himself. Painfully aware and resentful of the national penchant to turn a fast buck, he became furious whenever he discovered corrupt practices among his subordinates. He termed this tendency part of Vietnam's "colonial inheritance."

To charges that Diem was ruthless as a ruler, I affirm that I found him a highly moral and deeply religious man who agonized over the decisions he was forced to make. He would weigh endlessly the pros and cons, usually from the moral point of view. I sometimes found myself an unwilling audience to these deliberations, and I must bear witness to Diem's struggle to do what seemed right rather than what seemed politically expedient. I never felt that he was motivated by vindictiveness or cruelty, or that he enjoyed exercising power. He had wanted, Diem told me, to become a monk; in fact, in his youth he attended divinity school for a year. He chose politics because he felt that his country needed him.

Thus, despite its flaws, I continued to think that Ngo Dinh Diem's government was the best option available to lead South Vietnam and that with our help that government was slowing achieving its goals of stability, protection, and progress for its people. French reactions strengthened my convictions. The Michelin Company sent representatives who said, "Keep it up, this is working. We're not having as many rubber trees cut down, we're not having as many assassinations on our plantations." Representatives from other French and American industrial and commercial interests seconded these statements. Couve de Murville, the French Foreign Minister, twice invited me to his office when I was passing through Paris to Washington, just to give encouragement. This occurred during a low point in U.S.–French relations. France and our other NATO allies had known and respected President Eisenhower. His record as supreme commander of the allied forces during World War II and his willingness to consult and consider the views of NATO member countries helped establish and maintain these feelings. Although our European allies were attracted by John Kennedy's freshness, his dynamism, and his personal charm, they felt that he was untried as a national leader, less willing to consult with them on policy, and less reliable as an ally. There had been no consultation in NATO under the Kennedy administration on the Southeast Asia problem. While the French had not set a very good precedent on this, the United States had argued during the Eisenhower administration—I was on the NATO Political Consultation Committee, where this began—the benefits to be derived from constant consultation on political problems, no matter how thorny they might be. To have our government refuse to discuss the Vietnam issue was not good alliance diplomacy. The French also had something of a chip on their shoulder regarding Vietnam, because of their long involvement there. So I found it significant that Couve de Murville made a special effort to convey encouraging messages. He was careful, however, to make clear that he spoke for the French Foreign Office, not for President de Gaulle.

From most indications, my government shared this optimistic view. President Kennedy had been pleased with our progress when I had seen him in January 1962. After the first Secretary of Defense Conference in Honolulu in December 1961, we met with McNamara and other Vietnam policymakers nearly every month. We reviewed our actions and fine-tuned their execution, changing things here and there. The Secretary of Defense conferences were strenuous. After a long trip on a converted military tanker, we arrived in Honolulu to attend a series of meetings on various aspects of the problem. Some of these were military briefings, about the "junk fleets," the training of the ARVN, the roles of the U.S. advisors, and so forth. At the end, however, we generally had very frank, substantive discussions about how our efforts were going, where the "hearts and minds" of the people were. Each person had his own slightly different slant as to the loyalties and attitudes in one province or another, to what extent our programs were working well or not. Most of the participants, however, were optimistic; the conferences were generally upbeat.

As their name implies, Secretary of Defense McNamara chaired these meetings. This is significant in itself, for Vietnam was handled on a higher level in the Department of Defense than it was at State. I remember calling Dean Rusk about a specific problem, to find that he did not want to bother with it. He told me that he had more important things to deal with, like the Berlin crisis and other aspects of Soviet-American relations. "Dean, I appreciate that," I told him. "I realize Vietnam is a hangnail compared to your other problems. But it's likely to fester and give our body politic blood poisoning if you don't pay more attention to it." I do not recall specifically his response, but I do remember not engaging his attention.

McNamara and Defense filled a void in Vietnam policymaking. McNamara's energy and abilities were crucial to our efforts—and not on the military side alone. During his frequent visits to Saigon and Honolulu, he constantly urged us to make faster progress in helping to pacify and develop South Vietnam. On one occasion I said, "Bob, you're trying to put a Ford motor into a Vietnamese ox-cart. You will break it down!" But the New Frontier was not noted for its patience. It was our job to move things along as quickly as possible, and also to show Washington why progress could not be as speedy as it wished. McNamara was certainly enthusiastic in his support of our efforts. He once said, "Anything you want in the way of instruments, gadgets, or material, we can provide. We have everything. Don't hesitate to ask for it." This was after one of our discussions about the "hearts and minds" of the people, so I asked him, "Do you have a thermometer that I can take with me when I travel around the country, and use to see how a peasant feels about his government?" He shook his head, conceding, "No, you've got me there." But, aside from this, McNamara usually came through. In fact, his public statements following these conferences were so optimistic that they made me wince. Faced with day-to-day realities of the situation, we in Saigon were less euphoric than Washington. But we were encouraged and felt that we were making solid progress. Thus I wrote to Dean Rusk around Christmas 1962 reminding him of our conversation about the length of my tenure in Vietnam. I suggested that he might want to select my successor, so that we could begin an orderly transfer of responsibility in about six months.

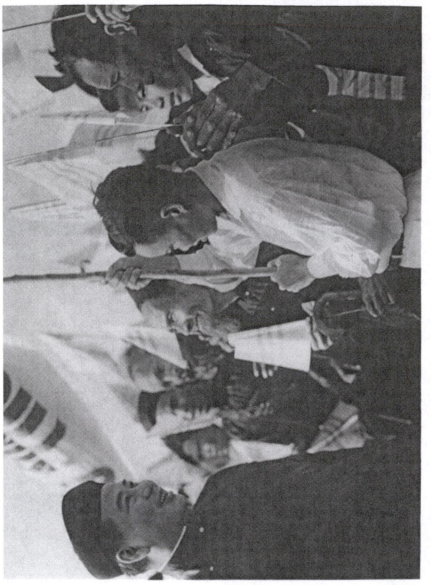

President Diem before a group of village elders and youth, LySon, 1961

The President asks questions of some village children, Mangbuk, 1961

Prominent ladies of state: Mrs. Lyndon Johnson, Madame Ngo Dinh Nhu, and Mrs. Jean Kennedy Smith, Saigon, 1961

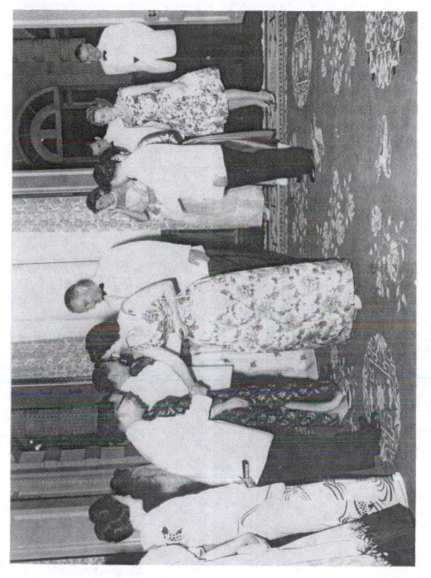

Vice President and Mrs. Johnson at President Diem's reception for them, May 1961

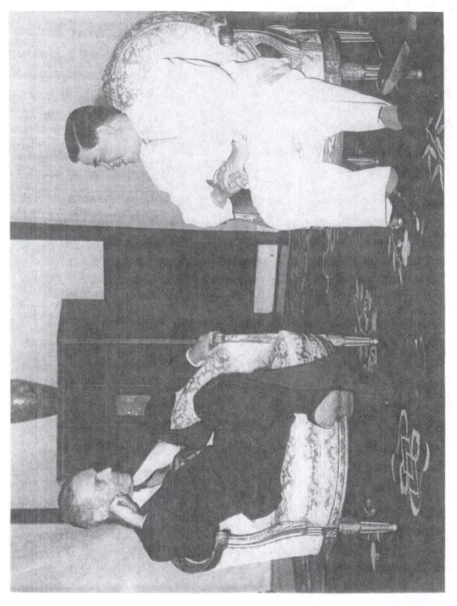

President Diem with General Maxwell Taylor, 1961

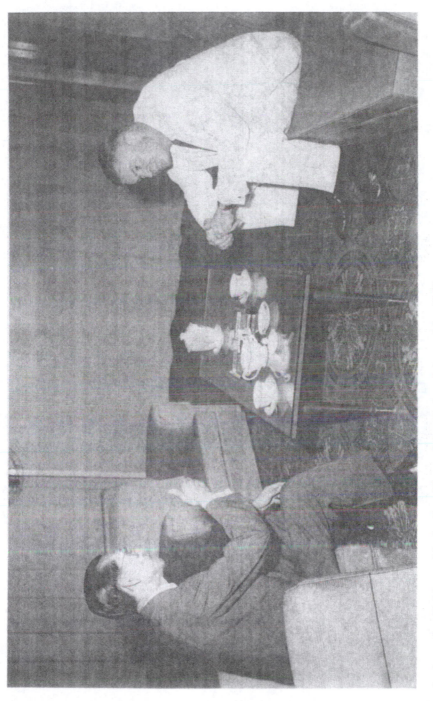

Ambassador Nolting with the President of the National Assembly, 1961

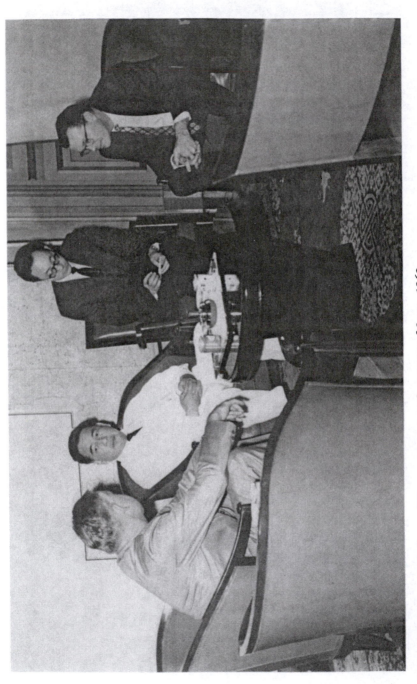

President Diem with Roger Hilsman, Assistant Secretary of State, 1962

Ambassador Nolting with Ngo Dinh Nhu at the Don Tin strategic hamlet, 1963

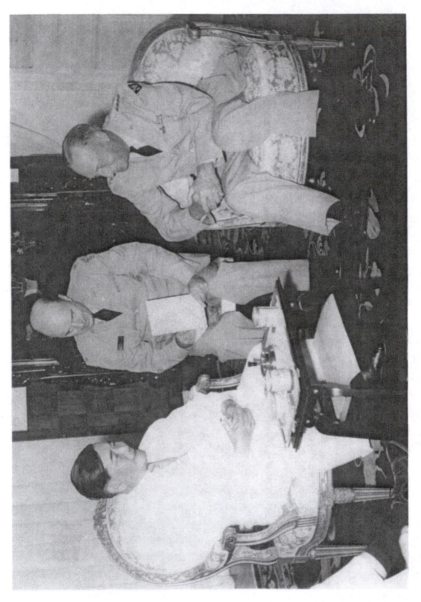

President Diem with General Paul Harkins, MACV, 1962

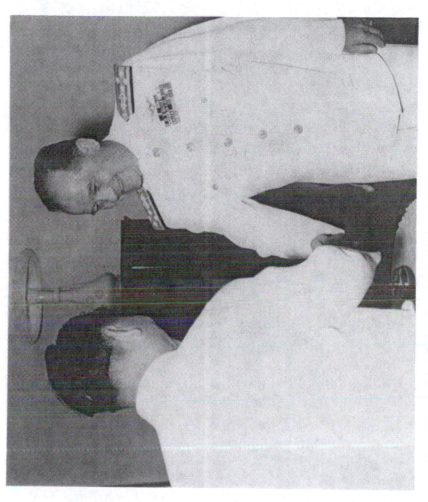

President Diem with Admiral Don Felt, CINCPAC, 1962

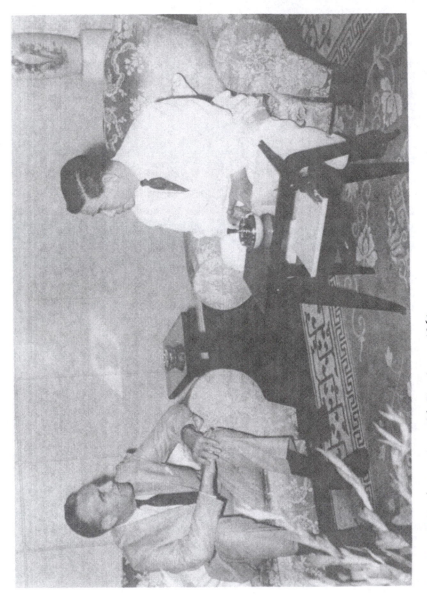

President Diem's meeting with Harriman, 1961

Lindsay Nolting at a center for undernourished children and orphans, Saigon, 1963

The Caritas Center after completion, Saigon, 1963

Note: Other similar projects promoting health and welfare were realized through the combined efforts and cooperation of Christians, Buddhists, the CVTC Labor Union, bonzes from nearby pagodas, Catholic nuns, the South Vietnamese government, and many volunteers, both civilian and military.

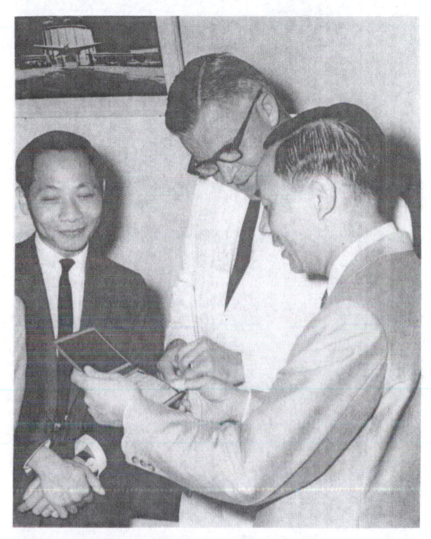

Ambassador Nolting presenting a check for the construction of the Atomic Energy Research Center to Minister Thuan, August 1963

President Diem and Ambassador Nolting at Nolting's farewell reception, 1963

Ambassador Nolting saying goodbye to President Diem, 1963

6

The Laos Accords, the Comprehensive Plan, and Media Relations

Ngo Dinh Diem was a stubborn man. So was Averell Harriman. The difference, it seemed to me, was that the one had intelligent reasons for his position and the other did not. They clashed first over the Laos treaty of 1962.

During the first year of the Kennedy administration, Harriman, as U.S. Ambassador-at-Large, was engaged in the extended negotiations in Geneva to reach an international agreement to secure the neutrality and territorial integrity of Laos. He retained this responsibility after he replaced Walter McConaughy as Assistant Secretary of State for Far Eastern Affairs in December 1961. Harriman's long career had included service as U.S. Ambassador to Moscow. He was reputed to be well qualified to conduct the negotiations in Geneva based on his experience in dealing with the Soviet Union. Although I did not know him well, I had always regarded him highly, having worked with him on European matters during the 1950s. It was Harriman who backed me when I returned from Saigon to Washington in January 1962 to protest the split mission envisioned in the creation of MACV, and he arranged the appointment with President Kennedy to resolve the matter.

Laos had been for years the victim of "nibbling" operations by the Communist Pathet Lao, supported by North Vietnam. President Kennedy first issued a stern warning to the Communists in 1961 threatening military intervention. Then he reversed himself and decided to seek a negotiated settlement. The objective was to seal off Laos from the arena of subversive war in Southeast Asia and to make it a neutral country—in effect, a little Switzerland. Harriman undertook to reach a solution of this kind by negotiations. A fourteen-power international conference was convened in Geneva, with Britain and the Soviet Union as co-chairmen, and the two sides (Communist and non-Communist) sat down to negotiate. Included were Thailand, the United States, Britain, Canada, the USSR, Burma, Cambodia, the People's Republic of China, the Democratic Republic of Vietnam (North Vietnam), the Republic of Vietnam (South Vietnam), France, India, Laos, and Poland. On our side, the aim was to achieve real neutrality, which meant the permanent withdrawal of all foreign forces from Laos and the prohibition of the use of Laotian territory for military purposes. A neutral government under Souvanna Phouma was to govern in all areas, including those controlled by the Pathet Lao.

The aims of the Communist countries at the conference were, as might have been expected, quite different. They wanted a treaty to tie our hands, but not theirs. The Ho Chi Minh Trail through eastern Laos was a valuable asset to them in supplying the Viet Cong, and they saw in these negotiations the opportunity to make it more secure for their purposes. As the negotiations wore on, Harriman (urged on by the British and French) gave one concession after another in order to reach an agreement on paper. The final provisions risked opening the Ho Chi Minh Trail to the North Vietnamese for infiltrating South Vietnam. Under the treaty, South Vietnamese forces were prohibited from crossing the Laotian border to stop the infiltration of supplies and military reinforcements into South Vietnam. CIA aid to the Meo tribesmen of Laos, who were attacking the infiltrators and who aided South Vietnamese interdiction operations, was to be terminated. The effectiveness of this agreement depended entirely on the good faith of the parties concerned. If Laos did not really become neutral, South Vietnam's flank would be exposed, its defense greatly endangered.

We followed these negotiations from Saigon with increasing misgivings. The South Vietnamese government had its own representatives at the Geneva Conference, and their reports to the Saigon government were even more alarming than those we received in Saigon from Washington. The idea of obtaining a real settlement in Laos was good, but the treaty that finally came out would make it more difficult to carry out the Kennedy administration's policy of supporting South Vietnam's independence. The Communist signatories had a long history of not living up to their agreements and probably would not do so in this case, since the treaty provided no effective means to enforce it. In Bangkok, too, the Thai government was becoming increasingly concerned as one safeguard after another was abandoned in the negotiations.

From time to time throughout the negotiations, Washington would ask us for our views on the way the Laotian treaty was developing. We sent back cables stating our reservations and those of the South Vietnamese government. I also discussed my concerns in person with Harriman at the regional ambassadors' conferences he chaired in Bangkok and Baguio. In response to my observations, Harriman told me he had a "fingertips feeling" that the Russians would enforce the agreements. His fingertips were those of an experienced hand in Soviet affairs. Even so, I said that my fingertips gave me precisely the opposite impression. During another discussion, Harriman stated that President Kennedy had "directed" him to get "a diplomatic settlement" on Laos, and that he was determined to do so. When I asked him whether the President knew the terms of the treaty and its total lack of safeguards, he did not answer directly, but said, "You're working for Kennedy, not God." At one point during these conversations, which became rather heated, I asked Harriman if he had ever read my instructions ordering our mission to work with the South Vietnamese government and to consider their views. He replied that he had not, but that he knew what he was doing.

Our objections in Saigon, as well as those of the U.S. Embassy in Thailand, had little effect. The American negotiators in Geneva, and their British and French colleagues, had their minds set on getting a settlement on paper. Such a treaty might or might not seal off Laos and make it a neutral country but would at least achieve President Kennedy's political aims. Finally, both South Vietnam and Thailand let it be known that they would not sign a treaty which rested entirely on the good faith of the Communist signatories, the very countries that were trying to subvert them. As neighbors of Laos, they had to live with the results of the treaty. A paper settlement would not be enough—they had to have secure borders or, failing that, no treaty. It was this incipient revolt that brought Averell Harriman to Saigon.

On September 20, 1961, in a small, steamy-hot room in the President's "Palace," Diem explained to Harriman at great length why he was unwilling to trust the Communist signatories to live up to their treaty obligations. Speaking through an interpreter, he went back to the early 1930s, tracing in some detail the history of Communist penetration into Southeast Asia, of agreements broken and bad faith displayed. He mentioned his personal experiences with Ho Chi Minh and the treachery of the Vienminh toward his older brother, whom they murdered. The historical record was impressively long and accurate. Its relevance to the question of signing the treaty on Laos without safeguards was clear.

But Harriman had turned off his hearing aid and closed his eyes. He appeared to be asleep. Diem noticed this with some annoyance but continued his monologue. Sitting next to Harriman on the sofa, realizing that he had had a long and tiring flight, I tried to nudge him into attention. Finally Harriman snapped, "I have a fingertips feeling, Mr. President, that the Russians will police this agreement and make the others live up to it. We cannot give you any guarantees, but one thing is clear: if you do not sign this treaty, you will lose American support. You have to choose." With that the meeting—a tough encounter—broke up. Shortly thereafter, Harriman flew back to Geneva.

On orders from Washington, I went to work to persuade President Diem, who was offended by the high-handed treatment he had received from Harriman, to sign the treaty in Laos. I told Diem that I thought he was in an awkward situation. President Kennedy clearly wanted a negotiated settlement in Laos. This seemed to be the best treaty possible, even though it was, in my opinion as well as his, inadequate, unprotected, and probably unenforce-able. Nevertheless, in order to maintain the full support of the Kennedy administration for the effort in South Vietnam, it would be better for him to sign the agreement.

Diem finally signed the accords. That proved to be a costly mistake, and I came to regret having urged him to do so. It soon became apparent that the Communist signatories, specifically North Vietnam, ignored the treaty's pro-visions from the beginning. Immediately after signing, the United States with-drew its assistance and advisors from the Laotian allies, the Meo tribesmen. The North Vietnamese, however, ignored the provision to remove their forces, as did the Communist elements within Laos, the Pathet Lao. Supplied with arms by the Soviet Union and China through North Vietnam, they never permitted Souvanna Phouma's government to send its officials into the Com-munist-controlled areas of eastern Laos. Harriman's "fingertips feeling" about Russian "policing" was not borne out by the facts. The Ho Chi Minh Trail, protected by the treaty from interdiction by our allies, was enlarged and developed by North Vietnam into a major route of infiltration into Laos, South Vietnam, Cambodia, and Thailand. Some called it the "Harriman Memorial Highway." Later, when the United States entered the war in force, our country became engaged in trying to knock out by bombing, at the sacrifice of many American lives, what was given away in negotiation.

The Declaration and Protocol on the Neutrality of Laos were signed at Geneva on July 23, 1962. At about the same time, General Harkins and I attended another Secretary of Defense Conference in Honolulu. The ill effects of the Laotian treaty had not yet become clear. The participants at the meeting agreed that our pacification and security efforts were proceeding well enough for us to begin preparing to withdraw some American military advisors. Secretary McNamara therefore directed our mission to develop a plan to reduce the American military presence in Vietnam. MACV first formulated the comprehensive plan, as our project came to be called, then coordinated its further development with our mission's Task Force. By the beginning of 1963, we had a concrete draft ready for Washington.

I have since read that the impetus for the comprehensive plan was political, that President Kennedy and his advisors wanted to be able to say before the 1964 elections that the United States had fewer Americans in Vietnam and that our involvement was decreasing. Pulling out a thousand or so advisors would dramatize this. This may have been a motive in Washington, but it was not our view in Saigon.

We believed sincerely that our training efforts had reached the point where they needed fewer Americans. Barring large increases in North Vietnamese infiltration, we felt that the Vietnamese could assume some of the duties of the American personnel and that the pacification program would continue to pick up steam under Vietnamese direction. We also felt, as did the South Vietnamese government, that the more we could shift these duties onto Vietnamese shoulders, the better. I do not recall any American officials at that time who thought we should involve ourselves more deeply in South Vietnam or bring in more Americans. Both the civilian and military elements at the mission believed the South Vietnamese government and military forces would be capable of standing on their own by the end of the five years during which our phased withdrawal would occur. In retrospect, this supposition may not have been correct. But it certainly was the prevailing view, and my own at the time.

This apparently was the thought in Washington military circles as well. The comprehensive plan was reviewed on several levels and ultimately endorsed by the Joint Chiefs of Staff. Eventually, the revised and endorsed plan was returned to the May 1963 Secretary of Defense Conference for implementation. During this meeting, Secretary McNamara spoke in concrete terms of pulling out at least a thousand American military personnel by the end of 1963. To me, this was not a cosmetic design but a true recognition of American success in Vietnam. Some civilian policymakers, however, did not share their military counterparts' sanguine outlook on Vietnam, as I learned during Senator Mike Mansfield's visit at the end of 1962.

Mansfield and his party, Senators J. Caleb Boggs, Claiborne Pell, and Benjamin A. Smith, arrived in Saigon on December 1, 1962. The Senate Majority Leader, Mansfield was considered something of an old hand on Southeast Asia. He was also a friend of President Diem, and he had been one of Diem's strongest supporters in Congress. His visit, which was managed by Mansfield's administrative assistant, Frank Valeo, began on a sour note. A monsoon developed while the party was in Thailand before its arrival in Vietnam. I sent a telegram to Senator Mansfield, saying that it might be dangerous in Saigon and asking him if he wished to delay his visit. I was referring only to the weather, but I think my message may have been misinterpreted as an attempt to wave off that visit. In any case, Mansfield seemed disgruntled when he arrived, apparently feeling that we did not welcome him and his mission.

Things did not improve during the next two days. The typhoon hit, but not as severely as anticipated, which may have led the group to believe they were right in thinking we did not want them there. A dinner President Diem was giving for his old friend was called off because of a disagreement about the seating list, creating more misunderstanding. Our visitors met briefly with the civilian and military representatives at the Embassy, but the briefing did not appear to interest them, and they asked few questions. Mansfield spent most of his visit meeting with journalists at his hotel. The other members of his party devoted little time to the mission or MACV.

Senator Mansfield said that he did not feel well and remained uncommunicative throughout his stay. The rest of his party seemed to share his mood. The negative attitude shown by Mansfield differed drastically from that of other Washington officials who had recently visited Saigon.

The Senators attended a reception held at our house on December 2, since we thought it would help morale if our people had the chance to meet the Majority Leader and the members of his party, but I do not think the evening was a resounding success. The morning of December 3 I called Mansfield at his hotel. He planned to leave that day, and I had hoped he would tell me generally what he intended to say in his parting statement at the airport. I spoke with Frank Valeo, who said that the Senator was unavailable. When I explained the reason for my call, Valeo stated curtly that he had no intention of discussing the statement, that Mansfield would "say what he wants to." His response gave me the impression that the group had discounted the Embassy's views and had made up their minds to blast Diem, in line with the journalists' views. As I surmised, Mansfield made a very negative statement at Ton Son Nhut Airport upon departure. Later, in his report to President Kennedy, he alleged that his old friend, President Diem, had lost contact with the people. I found his comments unfair and decidedly unhelpful to our relations with the South Vietnamese government.

I have no idea whether Mansfield came to Saigon as an objective observer or whether his mind was set on American politics rather than on the actual situation in Vietnam. I do feel that his appraisal reflected Frank Valeo's influence and the uneasy politics of Washington. His conversations with American journalists in Saigon were obviously persuasive to him. Senators Pell and Smith, whatever they thought, were submerged by the Majority Leader's views.

To speak of the American media in terms of a monolithic structure is, of course, absurd. The press and other media express various viewpoints, as they should. They reach different audiences, convey different impressions, feature different stories and pictures, carry different columns, express different editorial lines, employ writers and broadcasters of differing views. This diversity is surely a healthy characteristic of a free press. Even so, I have no doubt that the American media played a major role in undermining U.S. confidence in the Diem government. Was that justified?

Saigon from May 1961 to August 1963 was not the hotbed of journalism it would later become. Only a few American reporters were permanently assigned there. The reporters who did live in Vietnam represented the more powerful media—the *New York Times*, *Time* magazine, *Newsweek* magazine,

Associated Press (AP), United Press International (UPI), the Columbia Broadcasting Service, the National Broadcasting Company, and later the *Washington Post*. In my opinion, their influence was, to say the least, unfortunate. American public opinion about Vietnam was increasingly affected by a mere handful of reporters and broadcasters.

My relationship with the Saigon press corps began amicably. Soon after our arrival in Vietnam, the press representatives had a dinner party for us, and I spent a pleasant evening with five or six journalists. Unfortunately, my wife and best representative was not present because of her father's illness in Virginia. Homer Bigart of the *New York Times* was there, as was AP's Malcolm Browne. I believe Robert Trumbull, the senior *New York Times* man for the region, came over from Hong Kong. I do not recall if UPI's Neil Sheehan had come to Vietnam by then, but I do remember that a *Newsweek* representative attended. All in all, it was a congenial evening.

Why the situation deteriorated as it did, I do not know. Often I had handled press relations for the American delegation to NATO in Paris, and I had been reasonably successful. In fact, eminent journalists such as David Schoenbrun and Cy Sulzberger became respected friends as a result of this experience. But the atmosphere in Saigon was different. Perhaps we did not accommodate the members of the media, socially and otherwise, as much as they expected. My office was always open, and they came in frequently, both singly and in groups, and were occasionally at our home. But we had much to do, and I for one found it difficult to spend hours sitting down, having a drink, and discussing matters with members of the press, some of whom wanted individual interviews to give them a separate story.

I know that I underestimated the antipathy between Homer Bigart of the *New York Times* and the Diem government. Bigart was a distinguished journalist who had won a Pulitzer Prize before his assignment to Saigon. His feelings about the Diem regime were established and well known long before I arrived in Vietnam. While in Paris, I had read the telegrams my predecessor, Elbridge Durbrow, had sent describing his problems with Bigart. It was Bigart who coined the phrase "Sink or Swim with Diem" as a shorthand description of American policy in Vietnam. When I arrived, I found that Bigart's criticisms of the Diem government had deeply antagonized the regime. It was a serious situation, but I believed that if we got results, the facts would speak for themselves. Unfortunately, I was mistaken.

Bigart resented his "backwater assignment," as he termed Vietnam. I remember one occasion when he covered the opening of a vocational school in the provinces at which President Diem and I were present. After a brief ceremony, Diem, as was his custom, tramped around the countryside, looking at the rice paddies, the dikes, and the fish ponds, and talking with the people there. It was hot as hell, and the rest of the party was just slogging along behind him. I found myself walking beside Bigart, who was furious with the whole set-up. He did not like anything about it, and he made it clear that he most definitely did not want to be there.

Soon after that, I learned that Bigart's visa had expired and that the Vietnamese government had refused to renew it. On hearing this, I went immediately to President Diem, before I received Washington's instructions to do so. If Bigart was denied a renewal of his visa, I pointed out, it would be tantamount to the expulsion of the representative of America's leading newspaper. This could do nothing but harm to our mutual efforts. As expected, Diem used the occasion to pour out his grievances against the *New York Times* and its resident reporter. However, while I was in his office he telephoned the Minister of the Interior and directed him to renew the visa.

The next day Bigart called, saying that he would like to see me. I expected a word of appreciation, possibly even a change of attitude. Instead, he expressed considerable annoyance. He informed me that he had wanted to get away from his Vietnam assignment for some time and that his expulsion would have made his exit sensational. My intervention had only prolonged his stay and spoiled his story. I suggested that perhaps he, too, would have to "sink or swim with Diem" a while longer, but soon thereafter he was replaced by David Halberstam.

At first I thought Halberstam was a considerable improvement over Bigart. Though only twenty-seven when he came to Saigon, he impressed me as personable, eager, and energetic. But within a few weeks he was following the same line as his predecessor, perhaps more actively, finding things to criticize about the Diem government and very seldom, if ever, mentioning the good things it was doing. Halberstam quickly became the leader of the "get Diem" press group in Saigon. He did not use Bigart's phrase, but his articles implied that if we stuck with Diem, we would sink as if we were tied to a stone. Halberstam's considerable writing talent enhanced his influence. Beginning like drops of acid, his reports steadily conditioned the climate of American opinion. I suspect that Halberstam may have been catering to the *Times'* editorial line. He was, I think, influenced by his bosses and they by his reports, creating a crescendo of anti-Diem propaganda. This view is reinforced by a report I received from a trusted colleague just before I left Saigon in August 1963, ten weeks before the coup that overthrew and murdered the Vietnamese President. According to my colleague, Halberstam was at the Caravelle Bar, where newsmen often congregated, proudly displaying a telegram from his newspaper in New York, which said, in substance: "Good going. Keep it up. State Department is beginning to see it our way." I do not have the journalists' standard three sources to confirm it, but I believe that report.

Whatever its origin, Halberstam displayed an attitude of utter contempt for the Vietnamese government, as the following magazine excerpt illustrates:

A vast array of somewhat embarrassed Vietnamese in their white suits would show up in the office of then Ambassador Frederick Nolting, representing what was alleged to be the cabinet, knowing of course that they had no function or power, only to be amazed by their treatment from this foreigner. He quite clearly believed that the alleged foreign minister was, indeed, a foreign minister, that he deliberated long and hard on matters of state, that it was important to get him together with Rusk.[8]

On that rather foolish statement, I have two comments. First, no group of cabinet officers called on me in my office. If I had business with members of the cabinet, which I frequently did, I called on them in their offices, as any ambassador would do. Second, Vu Van Mau, the Foreign Minister at the time, did "deliberate long and hard on matters of state"—although I do not think he did so brilliantly, nor did I admire his later decision to shave his head during the Buddhist crisis. The quotation from Halberstam clearly reveals his attitude as well as his disregard of facts. The members of the South Vietnamese government, incidentally, heartily reciprocated his sentiments toward them.

I have commented at length on Bigart and Halberstam because, in my opinion, the *Times* did more than any other paper to influence the American public and government against Diem. On one occasion I sent Harding Bancroft, a ranking officer of the *Times* and a former State Department colleague, a clipping from our Foreign Broadcast Information Service in Saigon. It was a translation of a North Vietnamese broadcast to South Vietnam, which purported to be a *New York Times* editorial. It was so strongly critical of the Diem government that it was used by Hanoi radio to promote the overthrow of President Diem, the Communists' number one objective. In my note to Bancroft, I asked him whether this was, in fact, an editorial printed in the *Times*. After some time, I received a reply, enclosing a note from John Oakes, head of the editorial staff, in which Oakes said "Tell Nolting that we never printed such an editorial." Meanwhile, we had received the newspaper in Saigon and had found the editorial in question. Some of the words and phrases were different, because the editorial had been translated into the Vietnamese language for broadcasting from Hanoi and retranslated into English by our monitors. Whether or not Oakes realized this, I do not know. Still, the *Times*' anti-Diem editorials continued unabated. Later, the *Washing-*

ton Post picked up the same line, as did *Newsweek, Time,* and other publications.

Turner Catledge, the respected managing editor of the *New York Times,* visited Vietnam in 1962 to see for himself the situation there and to judge the *Times'* treatment of it. After several days of observation and conversations with many people, he told me that he thought his newspaper was wrong in its interpretations and mistaken in its editorial line about Vietnam. He said he was going back to New York to try to change things. No changes occurred. About two years later (after I had left the Foreign Service), Catledge asked me to lunch with him in New York. He said that he had done his best but could not prevail with the *Times* management. He just wanted me to know this. I admired his judgment and his frankness. I also wondered, then and now, who really sets the ideological line of the *New York Times.*

Neil Sheehan, the UPI representative in Vietnam, was an influential reporter. In a June 24, 1974, letter to the *Washington Post,* he said, "I was not in 1970 and am not now on anyone's 'side' in Indo-China." That statement is not consistent with his reporting from Saigon in my years there. I suppose it was his prerogative as a journalist, but his reports were certainly unsympathetic to the Vietnamese government and unhelpful to the American cause. More important, in my view they were often inaccurate reflections of a complex situation. The wire services, of course, were very important sources of information to thousands of newspapers in the United States, because there were so few resident reporters in Vietnam. They were, in fact, the only press sources for most papers in those years.

Malcolm Browne represented the AP. In my estimation, he was more sensitive to the nuances of the Vietnamese situation and therefore a more perceptive reporter than the other journalists I have mentioned. At the time of the Buddhist crisis, it was he who took the unforgettable picture of Tich Quang Duc, sitting as if in prayer while gasoline flames consumed his frail body. This picture won Browne a Pulitzer Prize. In Vietnam and America it created a wave of emotional hysteria which contributed to Diem's downfall. I do not blame Malcolm Browne for the picture, but I do blame the media (with a few notable exceptions) for their gullible misinterpretations following the old monk's pitiable immolation.

Other journalists were positive in their coverage of Vietnam. Marguerite Higgins was one, experienced, courageous, and outspoken. Keyes Beech, of the *Los Angeles Times,* and Joseph Alsop, and influential columnist, were generally supportive of U.S. policy in Vietnam. Various opinions about Vietnam were presented to the American public, but the major organs of the Eastern press, led by the *New York Times,* were increasingly negative.[9]

The U.S. mission and the Vietnamese government used the word "pacification" to describe the whole complex of our joint programs. The press used the word "war." To me this was not merely a question of semantics. It misinterpreted the whole thrust of our efforts. Military aspects were certainly a key to our endeavors, but they were not the entire program. Rather, they were the means necessary to stabilize the country, to make possible conditions under which our goal of liberalizing the government and strengthening its support could be achieved. The mission maintained that our military people were functioning as advisors. The journalists felt that we were splitting hairs. American advisors were getting killed, they pointed out; therefore, they must have been combatants. I believed, and still believe, that our distinction was valid. American military advisors were there to teach the Republic of Vietnam's armed forces the techniques they would need to win their struggle. These lessons could not be taught effectively from behind a desk in Saigon. Many of our people had to be with Vietnamese units in the field. It was dangerous, and, as a result, some died. Ninety-eight Americans were killed in the nine years from 1954 through 1963. But this did not mean that American soldiers were fighting the war. Sometimes brave, overzealous American advisors would take over from less experienced Vietnamese counterparts, piloting a plane or leading a unit. They would be reminded upon their return that this was not their role. The Vietnamese government was highly sensitive about such incidents, which were the exception rather than the rule. We tried to downplay them.

It was inevitable, I suppose, but unfortunate nevertheless, that the media focused their attention on the fighting. They were not interested in less dramatic events. When we went into the provinces to open a new hospital wing or a new educational facility built with American assistance, they seldom bothered to go. One particular health project of the Vietnam government used U.S. Operation Mission aid to add surgical wings to twenty-five provincial hospitals. These facilities cared for both military and civilian persons wounded in fighting with the Viet Cong. The United States had assembled medical teams of six people each from the United States, Canada, Australia, Sweden, the Philippines, and other countries to staff these hospitals. My wife, my children, and I participated in the formal openings of several such wings. These developments meant much to the people in the provinces and were concrete demonstrations of social benefits achieved through the joint U.S.– Vietnamese program.

The mission notified the press in advance about such events, inviting journalists to accompany us, but they rarely did. Two or three reporters leveled with me, saying that they could go, but their papers would not print the story; or if they did, it would be on the back page.

As early as February 1962, Washington issued new instructions on how the mission should handle the press. The telegram told us to take the journalists anywhere they wanted to go and to give them all the privileges and prestige possible. It said to give them spaces on helicopters, even if it meant depriving military or other essential personnel, and to do anything that would gain their confidence and support.

By and large, we found these instructions superfluous. General Harkins and I were doing our best already. We had frequent talks with reporters, giving them rides in short-supply helicopters so that they could see everything, and we explained the reasons for each operation, trying to get them to understand that our programs deserved more in-depth coverage than was offered.

Following the new instructions, I called a meeting of the resident press corps in my office. I said, "Gentlemen, I have received this message. I want to go over it with you." Then I described point by point what we could do for them. Instead of producing the intended effect, the meeting elicited a blast of criticism in the next day's papers against the U.S. government, particularly our mission and myself, for trying to "manipulate" the press.

As time went on, instructions to cultivate the media became more insistent. Washington, particularly the White House, was baffled and annoyed by the fact that U.S. efforts to support South Vietnam through its elected government were being undermined by constant press criticism of that government, casting doubts on U.S. policy. The White House could not understand it and continued to send us orders to "do something" about it.

As Ambassador I certainly was not successful with the press. I deeply regret that failure, but I wonder whether any amount of effort and skill would have changed the outcome materially. Paul Harkins initially got along well with the reporters, but his relationship with them deteriorated as time passed. John Mecklin, who joined the mission as a public affairs officer in 1962 and then replaced John Anspacher as Counselor for Public Affairs, was no more successful.

Mecklin was a former print journalist himself, whose experience included covering Indo-China from both Vietnam—he reported on the fall of Dien Bien Phu in 1954—and Europe. I believe he sincerely tried to promote official policy. I think, however, that he was torn by that policy and that, in the final analysis, he tended to agree more with his friends in the press than he did with his government. In this he may have been influenced by Neil Sheehan and David Halberstam, who lived in his house for quite a while after his wife left Vietnam to return to the States. Mecklin, however, never voiced his doubts in Saigon, although he had every opportunity to do so as a member of the mission Task Force. His book, *Mission in Torment*, revealed his dilemma. He seemed to feel that it was better to have a government policy supported by the press than an unpopular one that was consistent and reasonably successful.

I did not realize his true feelings until I heard his testimony before the National Security Council (NSC) in Washington in September 1963.

Overall, I felt that the American journalists in Saigon did too much of their "fact-finding" at the Caravelle Bar, where dissidents were eager to pass on to them the latest rumor about the malfeasance of the Diem government. Occasionally, they would go out into the countryside, but there again, they would often fail to put what they saw into perspective. A country at war is rife with tragic stories, displacements, apparent and real injustices. A reporter might choose, for example, to write up the story of a person allegedly mistreated by a province chief, and fail to convey the day-to-day struggle of the province chief himself to administer his area, under attack and under threat to his own life. The cumulative effect of such selective reporting, I felt, was an unjust and inaccurate picture of what the Vietnamese government was trying to do and what it was, in fact, accomplishing. Eventually, this undermined public support for U.S. policy in Vietnam.

There were many reasons why the views and reports of our mission in Saigon and those of the majority of the media were increasingly divergent. The United States, for better or worse, had undertaken a delicate and difficult policy in Vietnam. That policy involved helping a weak and sensitive country without throwing our weight around publicly. It involved working with a controversial government which was, after all, the only legitimate vehicle through which our aid could be channeled. South Vietnam was a country of extreme factions, political, social, and cultural. It was difficult for anyone unfamiliar with the country to realize the jealousies which existed among the more educated Vietnamese people, and the differences from province to province, region to region. These differences were, I think, partly a legacy of seventy-five years of French colonial rule. The greatest single problem of the Diem government was to bring about some degree of unity among the various non-Communist elements in the country. One of the main goals of the Viet Cong and Hanoi was to prevent this. The more Diem succeeded in giving South Vietnam a single identity, the more his overthrow became the Communists' principal objective.

In general, the American press, particularly the resident reporters in Saigon, looked to the U.S. mission to achieve a nearly impossible task: to transform a new and divided country into a unified democracy, Western-style, and to do so promptly. The United States was at that time spending about a million dollars a day ($350 million a year) in total aid to Vietnam, including military assistance. I remember this figure vividly, because I would think every morning on my way to the office, "What are we going to do with this million dollars today to make it worthwhile to the American people?" It was a lot of money. The press would point to it and ask, "Where are the results?" I do not claim we succeeded every day, or even every other day, but I firmly believe that on the whole, after 1961, things were getting better. "I think there are positive results," I said, "and you can see them. But if we plunge this country into a bigger war, the costs are going to be astronomical, and the results are going to be very uncertain."

Basically, the journalists who reported from Saigon were mistrustful and suspicious of the Diem government, its motives as well as its actions, and the regime certainly was responsible for some of its problems with the American press. I convinced President Diem to extend Homer Bigart's visa, but the regime did expel the Michigan State University Advisory Group from the country in February 1962. The MSU Group was not part of the press or of our mission. They were there on a private contract with the government of South Vietnam, mainly to advise on education. Their contract was terminated because several of their members published articles in the United States which Diem considered derogatory.

A huge cultural gap existed between the South Vietnamese people and the American reporters. At the Embassy we were almost as indignant as Halberstam himself when he came in sobbing over what was left of his camera, smashed in a melee with a Vietnamese policeman. But we saw the incident as one person's reaction in a tense moment, whereas Halberstam seemed to see it as a government-sponsored attack on the press.

Our mission was sent to help the South Vietnamese people through their elected government, while doing everything we could to improve the government's performance. We had to do this by advice and persuasion, not by trying to assume authority over it. Obviously, this entailed a certain reticence in talking about American accomplishments. Often we discussed this rationale with the reporters, whom it did not satisfy. They thought we were backing the wrong horse. Yet when we asked them, "If you do not think we are on the right track, what alternative policy or program do you suggest?", they produced no constructive answers. They spoke of "democratic reforms," without specifying what they meant by the phrase or what could be done to achieve them. In general, they took the position that it was their function to diagnose the patient, ours to cure him.

Although serious, Harriman's dispute with Diem over the Laos accords, the pall Senator Mansfield's visit cast, and our problems with the press fell into the fabric of our everyday life and work. They seemed at the time merely problems that arise in any difficult job.

7

From Euphoria to Ferment

By early 1963, Washington was in a mood of euphoria about Vietnam. South Vietnam, with limited American help, seemed to be winning its long struggle against subversion. Press criticism had abated somewhat, and our government was genuinely encouraged. In Saigon we were encouraged too. But the records show that our people on the spot were less euphoric and more cautious than Washington was. While the areas under GVN control in most regions were enlarging, giving impetus to social and economic improvements among the people, we realized that the momentum could change, particularly if there were increased infiltration of men and weapons from North Vietnam to the Viet Cong, or direct invasion from North Vietnam.

At about that time I wrote to Secretary Rusk again, referring to our conversation in May 1961 and suggesting that he consider selecting my successor to set in motion an orderly transfer while things were on the upswing. In due course I received a reply from Harriman, citing the progress that had been made and instructing me to stay on the job indefinitely. I believe it was in this exchange that Harriman suggested that my wife and I take a vacation some time in the spring or summer.

A visit by Roger Hilsman and Michael Forrestal occurred at that time. Hilsman was the Director of Intelligence and Research in the State Department. Forrestal was the National Security Council's specialist on Vietnam who functioned as the NSC liaison with Harriman. They arrived in Saigon at the end of 1962 and stayed into the new year.

I did not know it at the time, but Hilsman and Forrestal's visit was spurred by a private, extremely negative report Senator Mansfield had given to President Kennedy upon his return from Vietnam. Nothing in our talks with Hilsman indicated this, or that Washington was changing or preparing to change its policy toward South Vietnam and the Diem government. Hilsman and Forrestal showed the usual concern about speeding up progress, as other administration visitors had done. There had been substantial progress in 1962, they acknowledged, but the U.S. presidential elections were approaching, and the administration wanted faster improvement. The President was worried about spending $350 million a year on Vietnam, they said, and especially about the media's dim view of our progress and policies.

Hilsman seemed quite optimistic during this visit, Forrestal less so. I was never quite sure where Mike Forrestal stood. He came out to Vietnam occasionally, did not say much, did not appear to do much, then returned to Washington. He reported to the President through the NSC rather than through the State Department, so I did not see his reports, but during our discussions we sometimes disagreed on priorities. Forrestal, echoing Harriman, urged more democratic institutions and methods, pressing Diem to broaden the base of his government and become more "popular." I perceived such comments to be unrealistic and impossible to accomplish in a short time under existing conditions. I am sure Washington found me stubborn when I reported in this vein.

Forrestal spent a lot of time with American press representatives during this trip, gathering, I suppose, what he thought was "inside information," untainted by the Embassy. In the end, however, neither he nor Hilsman suggested anything substantial in terms of changing our policies or programs. Their final report, which I did not see until it was published in the *Pentagon Papers* in 1965, was generally positive, saying that there was more to be done and that it could be done at a faster pace, but that, overall, things seemed to be going well. They left on a positive note, even though they were in Saigon during the setback that arose over Ap Bac.

The Battle of Ap Bac occurred on January 1, 1963, when the Viet Cong engaged an ARVN force near the village of Ap Bac. Although the ARVN unit outnumbered its enemy and had superior firepower, the Viet Cong inflicted heavy casualties and destroyed five helicopters. Afterwards, Colonel John Paul Vann, and American military advisor, told the press that despite all the Americans had done to train and supply them, the members of the South Vietnamese Army were basically cowards who could not win. Allegations also arose that President Diem had ordered the Army to avoid casualties and that because of these orders ARVN commanders were not taking the initiative in combat.

General Harkins and I agreed that the South Vietnamese forces mishandled Ap Bac. They did not move in when they should have. We did not think, however, that the entire South Vietnamese Army deserved to be indicted for cowardice. Colonel Vann, who later gave his life in Vietnam, caused great damage by his press interview. His outburst stemmed, no doubt, from genuine frustration, but it was unfair to the South Vietnamese Army and government and did great harm in terms of American public opinion.

No one, not President Diem, not Paul Harkins after his many talks with

Diem, not Nguyen Dinh Thuan, the effective Defense Minister, ever said or intimated to me that the South Vietnamese government was ordering the Army to hold its punches. I never saw or heard of any orders to avoid combat. I do recall many discussions with Diem and other officials who thought that the fewer the casualties among the Army, the villagers, the fence sitters, and even the Viet Cong, the sooner pacification of the countryside could take place. Both the Vietnamese armed units and their American advisors were instructed to be careful about whom they attacked, since we wanted to bring dissenters over to our side, not kill them. There were mistakes in tactics and judgment, of course, but they were the exception rather than the rule.

The press accusations that many operations were launched to avoid, rather than engage, the enemy were to my knowledge false. To be sure, President Diem, his cabinet, and MACV were strongly opposed to killing innocent people while trying to root out terrorists. In some cases Diem reprimanded his generals for attacking villages whose allegiance was in doubt. In addition to humanitarian considerations, neither the Vietnamese government nor the American mission wanted to put the fence sitters on the Viet Cong side, but killing innocent civilians.

Ap Bac was, in my view, a relatively small battle which the American press blew out of proportion, partly because of Colonel Vann's statements. It stimulated the media's rhetorical chant, "Why aren't our Vietnamese as good as their Vietnamese?" I think that, overall, they were as good. There were far more successful military actions than there were debacles like Ap Bac. These successful battles did not make dramatic headlines because we expected our side to win. Americans in the early 1960s did not envision military setbacks, even on the part of our allies at a time when we were not engaged as combatants. The media tended to feature the setbacks, creating a false impression of the ARVN's capabilities and of American training and advice.

Hilsman and Forrestal's trip was followed by a visit at the end of January by Army Chief of Staff General Earle G. Wheeler and General Victor Krulak, Special Assistant for Counterinsurgency on the Staff of the Joint Chiefs of Staff. Like Hilsman and Forrestal, President Kennedy had sent them to investigate the allegations in Mansfield's private report, from the military side. We found nothing unusual in their visit or in the reexamination of policy it entailed. We were constantly reevaluating policy at the mission, either on our own initiative or as a result of instructions from Washington. General Krulak did not indulge in public statements, as some of our other official visitors did, but his thinking was sound and his advice practical. Both he and General Wheeler appeared quite positive in their assessments of the military situation.

Thus 1963 began positively, continuing the previous year's progress. The

Hilsman/Forrestal and Krulak/Wheeler visits reinforced our feelings that we were on the right track. Early in the year we completed a draft of the comprehensive plan for gradual American withdrawal from Vietnam and forwarded it to Washington. The pacified areas in the country continued to expand, government services to the people continued to increase and improve, and the Strategic Hamlets program appeared to be consolidating these gains. The infiltration rate from North Vietnam was estimated at less than 500 a month.

Then, in March 1963, the Senate Foreign Relations Committee released the report Senators Mansfield, Pell, and Smith had made on their trip to Vietnam. It was very negative, alleging that President Diem had closeted himself away from the people, was looking progressively inward, and had become increasingly dependent on his family. It called on Diem to broaden his government and to introduce democratic reforms without delay.

Mansfield's report wounded President Diem deeply. He asked me to come to his office, where he told me that he was not going to let it end his friendship with Mansfield, but that he thought the report was unfair. Diem knew enough about the American political system to discriminate between a Senate Foreign Relations Committee report and a statement of U.S. policy, but he was concerned about the report's impact on President Kennedy. I personally thought Mansfield's report did a great disservice to the government and our cause in South Vietnam. It encouraged the non-Communist dissidents against the regime, thereby diminishing, rather than increasing, the chances of broadening the government. It gave the Viet Cong a bonanza; they could see support for Diem and his government weakening in the United States. In retrospect, I consider the Mansfield report the first nail in Diem's coffin. Diem was right to fear its effect on President Kennedy and other policymakers in Washington.

The Mansfield report was the first real indication we had in Saigon of negative thoughts in Washington about our policy in Vietnam. Officially, however, it had little effect. Our instructions remained unchanged. We were still to create confidence between the United States and the Diem regime and use that confidence to achieve greater liberalization of the government and social improvements to help strengthen South Vietnam's military forces and its economy. The report's psychological impact on the South Vietnamese government, however, made it harder for us to do our job. It shook the confidence we had built between the mission and the regime, making it more difficult to persuade the government to do things that might have broadened its base of power and strengthened it in the long run.

The Diem government, always sensitive about Vietnam's prerogatives as a sovereign nation, became even more touchy about anything it perceived as interference in the country's internal affairs. It may have been coincidence, but it was at this time that Counselor and Madame Nhu began their strident campaign to reduce the American presence in Vietnam, making it more difficult for our mission in Saigon to deal with both the Diem and U.S. governments.

In a tragedy-laden chapter of Vietnamese history dominated by two strong men, Ho Chi Minh and Ngo Dinh Diem, the two people most fascinating to the American public seem to have been Monsieur and Madame Ngo Dinh Nhu. As a couple, and individually, their lives had a profound influence on the destiny of their country.

Madame Nhu, a vivid and extremely pretty woman, was married very young to a man much older than herself. She had little formal education in the Western sense, but she had extraordinary vitality and energy. Being young, photogenic, and only too willing to talk, she was a natural target for the press. Her command of English seemed much greater than it was (she never used English in private conversation if there was a choice), and while her indiscreet public pronouncements influenced history, I think that she did not understand the implications of some of her own outrageous remarks.

Madame Nhu came from a wealthy Buddist family and converted to Catholicism at the time of her marriage to Ngo Dinh Nhu. Her father was enraged when some of his large land holdings in the South were distributed to peasants under Diem's land reform program (the land was paid for, but not to his satisfaction). He became a bitter enemy of the Diem government, and Diem, with incredible naivete, tried to solve the family friction by appointing him Vietnam's Ambassador to Washington.

All of this occurred before my appointment to Saigon, but there were indications of family friction before. Ambassador and Mrs. Tran Van Chuong gave a dinner for my wife and me at their embassy in Washington before we left for Vietnam. They were gracious, but we were struck by their absence of enthusiasm for the South Vietnamese cause and the government in Saigon. They (Ambassador Chuong in particular) seemed to avoid the subject. I remarked on this to a State Department colleague who said, in effect, not to worry about it; Ambassador Chuong was not influential in Washington.

Later, on a visit to Saigon, Ambassador Chuong called and asked to see me. He used the occasion to pour out his grievances against the Diem government. I questioned him closely. He did not want to give up his job in Washington or return to Vietnam. He thought his daughter had made a terrible mistake in casting her lot with the Ngo family, which he scorned. In the final analysis, however, his grievance came down to money and property. He was bitterly opposed to the land reform program as it affected him, a rich absentee landowner. I remarked that the land reform program was something the U.S. had strongly advocated for years as a measure to win the peasants' support.

In my opinion, I said, there was too little land reform, not too much. If his country was to be saved from the Viet Cong, he should support it.

The same evening, as chance would have it, we had invited for dinner Ambassador and Madame Chuong, together with the Ngo Dinh Nhus and several members of the Vietnamese government. When they arrived, my wife took Madame Nhu aside and asked her whether she would mind if her mother and father were seated at the places of honor. "Of course not," she replied. "That's exactly how we would do it at home." It turned out to be a very congenial evening—no politics and no trace of friction. In fact, the "First Lady" and Ngo Dinh Nhu went out of their way to make it so.

On the public side of her character, Madame Nhu was autocratic, proud, and very much a center-stage person. She was also intelligent, innovative, and determined to promote the rights and opportunities of women in South Vietnam. She organized the Women's Solidarity Movement with the aim of making legal, medical, and simple domestic advice available to all women in the country who might need or want it—an ambitious cause but certainly a good one. She also organized a woman's Volunteer Militia as a supplement to the Home Guards in the villages and hamlets. As a member of Parliament, she vigorously promoted these causes. While there were a number of women in Parliament who had more formal education than she did and felt more qualified for leadership, Madame Nhu considered herself the leader of the feminist movement and did not let anybody forget it. The resulting resentments were inevitable. In sum, I think Madame Nhu sincerely wanted to help the women of her country and in this was successful, given the circumstances. I also think that while she wanted to dominate her husband and her brother-in-law, she was far less successful in this than the public was led to believe.

The last time my wife and I saw Madame Nhu was the night after her beloved and talented elder daughter, Le Thuy, was killed in a motor accident south of Paris in 1966. Madame Nhu called us for comfort in her distress. We were then resident in France, and we spent several hours with her. She blamed herself then for what she called her sin of pride and its contribution to her family's tragedies. Given the murder of her husband, the loss of her country, and the sudden death of her gifted child, one really cannot now be interested in old rumors like those repeated in Stanley Karnow's *Vietnam: A History*, or in the Vietnamese jealousies or the intrigues in Saigon's upper-class society.

Ngo Dinh Nhu was a more complicated person, in my judgment. A scholar by preference, he was engaged in an intensive work on Vietnamese history at the University of Hanoi when he and his wife became refugees in 1954 and fled to the South, leaving all their possessions, including his manuscripts, references, and notes, which were destroyed.

A native of Annam, the central province of old Vietnam, he was a strong anti-Communist patriot. I knew Ngo Dinh Nhu mainly through unofficial contacts—hunting trips, occasional social gatherings, and the like. With me, he never put himself forward as a spokesman for the government. Unlike Attorney General Robert Kennedy, he held no official position. But like Bobby Kennedy, he was considered to be (rightly, I think) his President's closest advisor. I called him "Mr. Counselor" and he called me "Mr. Ambassador." He spoke occasionally of his disagreements with his brother, President Diem, and more often about the differences with his brother Ngo Dinh Can in Annam and his eldest surviving brother, Archbishop Ngo Dinh Thuc, the head of the Catholic Church in South Vietnam. None of this seemed to be politically serious—more in the nature of family differences of opinion.

Nhu was an avid tiger hunter and a crack rifle shot. On two occasions, I went tiger hunting with him. Tiger hunting used to be simple in Vietnam before the Viet Cong insurgency. One built a blind in a likely place, baited a strip of forest with a dead deer, and waited for a tiger. But by the time I got to Vietnam, that procedure was dangerous—not because of tigers but because of Viet Cong snipers. So Nhu and I hunted at night with miners' spotlights on our foreheads. A yellowish reflection from the eyes of an animal in the underbrush signaled a deer or some member of the bovine family, possibly a stray water buffalo. A reddish reflection indicated a tiger or some other member of the cat species. We walked long hours, seeing many animals' eyes, but seldom shot. I remember two deer killed, a large skunk-like animal, a huge bobcat, but no tigers. After a hunt, we stretched out on blankets on the ground—it got chilly in the mountains. Nhu talked at great length about the future of a free Vietnam. He was an interesting talker, but finally I fell asleep when the subject turned to "Personalism."

On that subject, I had "had it" years before as a student of philosophy (particularly Aristotle, whose views in some respects resembled those expounded by Nhu). But there is one observation I want to make. "Personalism" was not a doctrine directed toward oligarchy or family rule, as was frequently implied in the press. On the contrary, it was a doctrine of individual development, self-realization (together with self-sacrifice), and Confucian social compassion. Quoting Aristotle, I said to Nhu, "You mean that the essence of man is to strive to be human." With some elaborations, he agreed.

Whatever others may think of Ngo Dinh Nhu, I consider him a Vietnamese patriot who, in his own way, did his utmost in the cause of a free Vietnam and died bravely in the attempt. For Madame Nhu and her surviving children one can now have only profound sympathy and compassion.

In diplomacy I think there is a great difference between firmness and what Senator Fulbright called "the arrogance of power." I cite two instances, both having to do with the Ngo Dinh Nhus. At a conference of American regional ambassadors at Baguio called by Averell Harriman, while some fifteen of us were seated at a long table, the chairman, Harriman, was handed a telegram from Saigon. It contained a description of another "anti-American" speech made by Madame Nhu. Harriman read it and passed it down the table with a note to me: "Nolting—what are you going to do about this b—ch?" I passed it back with a note: "What would you propose, *Sir*?"

Actually, as Harriman knew, I had on several occasions intervened with President Diem to stress to him the unfortunate effects of Madame Nhu's speeches on American public and official opinion. Diem understood this and was himself annoyed and worried by her speeches. He wanted her to control her tongue but added that, as a member of Parliament, she was free to express her own views. I said that her position was ambivalent; as his official hostess she was more than a member of Parliament and, besides, she was a lightning rod for the press. Finally, Diem asked me to talk with her husband about the matter, which I did immediately (Diem having telephoned Nhu from his office). In that frank exchange, Ngo Dinh Nhu promised to do what he could to restrain his wife, but I was not reassured that he could (or would) do much.

Soon thereafter, I received through CIA channels a copy of a speech Madame Nhu was scheduled to make in a few days. It was more of the same—"Don't let the Americans take over our country! Resist American pressure! Beware of American culture and moral values, especially you women of the Solidarity Movement." I picked up the telephone and called President Diem in Hue, where he was visiting his mother, and told him about Madame Nhu's proposed speech. He said, "How do you know about it?" "I can't tell you, Mr. President, but it's a fact—and I'm sure you remember our discussions on this subject." Diem sighed and said, "Thank you for letting me know."

A half hour later, Madame Nhu telephoned. She was furious. "Did you speak with the President in Hue?" she asked. "Yes, I did, today." "Well, he has just *ordered* me not to make that speech!" Whereupon she hung up.

The sequel to this incident is revealing of her temperament. She telephoned again in a few days. "You were absolutely right about the speech," she said cordially. "I was thinking in terms of Vietnamese culture, not Vietnamese-American relations. I was wrong. I will try to be more discreet."

Unfortunately, she did not stick with her resolution, especially after the outbreak of the "Buddhist crisis." But, by contrast, I never heard Harriman apologize for his rudeness.

There was other more substantial business to attend to in Saigon. Under instructions from Washington, the Embassy had been negotiating with the South Vietnamese government since February 1963 to obtain joint control over the "Counterinsurgency Fund." This fund comprised both counterpart funds—monies generated by U.S. imports—and contributions from the Vietnamese government. It was used to finance counterinsurgency programs, especially the Strategic Hamlets program. There was precedent for our proposal, since counterpart funds were already jointly controlled, and the United States had to approve all expenditures from them. The difference in this case was that South Vietnam was contributing to the Strategic Hamlets fund through its government's budget.

We presented a proposal to the President's office for joint U.S.-Vietnamese control of the Counterinsurgency Fund, noting that the United States intended to increase contributions to it. Neither Minister Thuan, to whom we conveyed the request, nor I saw anything unusual in it. The negotiations proceeded smoothly until April, when the agreement was ready for President Diem's signature. Diem refused to sign, saying that to do so would give the United States control over South Vietnam's budget, in essence reducing the government to colonial status in his view. It soon became apparent that Nhu shared his brother's stance. South Vietnam would consult with us about specific expenditures and discuss them, but would not give the United States veto power over its budget. The Vietnamese government framed its objections clearly as a matter of national sovereignty, something it absolutely would not concede.

In connection with this controversy, I sent a telegram to Washington, pointing out that Diem's position on this matter came close to a repudiation of his original agreement in 1961, on which our entire program of aid and advice rested. I recommended a series of measures to bring him around, including a suspension of financial aid if it came to that. It was strong medicine, but it worked. I never had to use the threat of sanctions, as it turned out. Through Thuan, Diem got the message of our firmness on this issue, and after a further exchange he agreed to our position.

On May 17, 1963, our Embassy and the Diem government issued a joint communiqué "regarding the funding for counter-insurgency and other economic development projects, particularly those supporting the Strategic Hamlet Program, during 1963." "The agreement," the communiqué continued, "provides *inter alia* for the continuation of counter-insurgency projects supported under the piastre-purchase agreement announced in August 1962." The communiqué also noted that "although at this time the present level of the advisory and support effort is still necessary, as the security situation improves and as the strategic hamlet program progresses, it is expected that the need for foreign assistance, both in terms of material and personnel, will be progressively lightened."

This controversy and its resolution made little impression on me, perhaps because I viewed it as routine, perhaps because subsequent events overshadowed it. I have since learned, however, that it had tremendous impact in Washington, to the point that the National Security Council was scheduled to discuss it. The discussion never took place, apparently deferred for more pressing issues, but this was the first time in 1963 that Vietnam appeared on the NSC agenda. President Kennedy and his advisors were to examine—I learned later—whether the United States could continue active support of the Diem government and the counterinsurgency effort in Vietnam if we did not get joint control of this fund. This dispute deepened Washington's perception that Diem was a difficult person to deal with and enhanced its impression that Nhu was even more stubborn than his brother. Washington viewed Nhu as the person behind Diem who was arguing that the United States was assuming too large a presence in Vietnam. Even though Diem eventually signed the agreement, the argument left a bad taste in officialdom's mouth. These events and feelings may have factored into a reevaluation of Vietnam policy, and into Washington's opinion of how the mission—I in particular—handled Diem.

None of this ferment reached us in Saigon, although throughout the first months of 1963 we did perceive subtle indications of changes in attitude, particularly in State and the White House. The mission would occasionally receive a message to do something quite contrary to our original instructions, such as "cultivate the opposition to President Diem." In response, I would cable the Department requesting clarification. Did the message mean to get to know the members of the opposition? The Embassy had already done that. We knew who opposed President Diem. I had met these people and had talked often with them, as had my colleagues. Or did the Department want the Embassy to give a sign that the United States was interested in seeing the opposition become an active alternative to the Diem government? In that case, this was a very serious change in policy, which I questioned strongly. How were we to "cultivate the opposition" and at the same time maintain influence on the present government? This simply would not work, given Diem's suspicious nature. Furthermore, it would constitute interference in Vietnam's internal politics. Through me, President Kennedy had in 1961 promised expressly not to use our increased aid as leverage to interfere in South Vietnam's internal affairs.

The matter faded for the time being but cropped up again after Roger Hilsman became Assistant Secretary of State for Far Eastern Affairs. (Harriman became Under Secretary of State for Political Affairs on April 4, 1963. Hilsman was appointed to replace him in FE (Assistant Secretary for Far Eastern Affairs) on April 25 and took office May 9.) Receiving a personal letter from Harriman suggesting that we "cultivate the opposition," I replied in the same vein as before. My point was that Diem had been reelected to the Presidency in 1961.

The Vietnamese people had the opportunity and right to change their government by constitutional means. But unless our instructions were changed formally, we were to work with the elected government, not undermine it. It therefore seemed inconsistent to me to cultivate the opposition in the sense that some people in Washington suggested. The political situation was too volatile for that.

I attributed such informal signals to the gradual coming into power of people under Harriman's influence with a different slant on Vietnam, rather than to a considered change in policy. I realized that there were dissenting factions in Washington. There were people who had maintained that U.S. policy could never succeed in Vietnam as long as Diem headed the government. The original presidential Task Force report had overruled them in 1961, while the progress achieved in 1962 silenced them further. I was aware also of Harriman's antipathy toward Diem and his family, a legacy of the Vietnamese President's reluctance to sign the Laos accords. I knew Harriman had supporters and sycophants in the State Department. But so far as we knew in Saigon, no formal review had been given to changing the mission's instructions. I had also received several private letters from Hilsman assuring me that he was his own man, that he would be calling the signals on Vietnam policy, and, in effect, not to worry about the "Old Crocodile," as some called Harriman. I remember thinking that perhaps the new Assistant Secretary was protesting too much, but the fact remained that Washington did not officially alter our course.

No doubt I underestimated Harriman's influence, tenacity, and vindictiveness. I never envisioned that he would carry his grudge against Diem to the extent that he did. Nor did I think that he would develop a grudge against those of us who supported the South Vietnamese President as the best available leader. I knew Mike Forrestal shared Harriman's views, but it was not until the May 1963 Secretary of Defense Conference in Honolulu that I realized that what I had viewed as isolated incidents involving individuals carried much broader significance.

As the conference participants discussed the comprehensive plan, which Defense and the Joint Chiefs of Staff had revised and returned to Saigon for implementation, I began to develop suspicions about exactly who was backing whom on Vietnam. Some of those present expressed views about a change in the South Vietnamese government, or at least "cultivating the opposition." Hearing this from Harriman did not surprise me, but I did not expect it from Robert Hilsman. After one of these sessions, I privately asked Alex Johnson, "What goes on here? Am I hearing that our policy has been changed?" As Deputy Under Secretary of State for Political Affairs, U. Alexis Johnson had regularly attended the Honolulu meetings since their inception. He represented the State Department's highest professional echelons and should have known the answer to my query. He responded unequivocally: there was no cleavage on policy between Washington and Saigon; no change of policy had occurred or was to be expected in Washington. As we walked up and down the beach, he assured me that our program in Vietnam was on an even keel, that I would, of course, be advised if there was any change in policy.

On balance, the progress being made in Vietnam still outweighed negative factors in Washington such as the Mansfield report and Harriman's ascendancy in the administration's policymaking. The job was still getting done in Vietnam. The sensible thing to do, I believed, was to continue on course.

Then came the beginning of a major crisis. On May 6, 1963, soon after I returned to Saigon from meetings in Honolulu, President Diem directed that the Vietnamese flag be given precedence over religious banners flown in public displays. He issued the order in response to the prominence given the Vatican flag at a recent Catholic celebration in Hue. Two days later, a large crowd assembled in Hue to celebrate the birth of Gautama Buddha. Buddhist flags were displayed ahead of the national flag. As the crowd attempted to take possession of the radio station, Vietnamese troops were called in by the province chief to enforce the recent decree and to protect the radio station. The demonstration became violent. Several shots (or explosions) occurred. Eight people died.

It was never determined beyond doubt whether these deaths were caused by the Army unit involved or by plastic bombs thrown by agitators. From the evidence I saw, I think both were involved: shooting by the Army and one or more bombs thrown by agitators into the crowd. The Buddhists charged religious persecution. President Diem ordered an immediate investigation into the incident, assigning the Minister for the Interior, Bui Van Luong, this task.

The incident was deplorable in itself and more deplorable because of its time-fused effect. It was also surprising to most Vietnamese people I talked to about it. Why, they asked, did this incident have to occur at a time when morale and national progress seemed good? Why did the government call in troops? Why did the crowd try to seize the radio station? Most important, who *was* responsible for the deaths of eight people? These questions remain largely unanswered to this day.

In my view, there is no doubt that the government officials at Hue acted unwisely in the first instance. The enforcement of a recent decree (probably unknown to most of the crowd) should not have required the use of Army forces. The attempt to seize the radio station, however, was not in the nature of a peaceful religious demonstration. It was illegal and smacked of political motives by agitators. Yet no one at the time really knew the facts, the motives, or the consequences of this deplorable event.

Without attempting either to condemn or justify the actions of either side at Hue on May 8, I would like here to give my view of the role of religions in Vietnam, before this incident inflamed the country. A wide spectrum of religions was represented in Vietnam, from Buddhism to ancestor worship to Christianity to the Hoa Haos and other sects. A very few "Westernized" persons sneered at Buddhism and other Asian forms of worship, but most Vietnamese held a Confucian attitude toward religion. Confucius stood for religious toleration, and this concept generally transcended all religions in Vietnam, as well as any differences they may have engendered. In many houses one would find a Buddhist shrine in one corner and a Christian shrine in another corner of the same room. There was very little, if any, religious intolerance in South Vietnam.

President Diem was himself a devout Roman Catholic. The other members of his family also practiced this faith. Madame Nhu had converted from Buddhism to Roman Catholisism upon her marriage to Ngo Dinh Nhu. An older brother of the President, Ngo Dinh Thuc, was Archbishop of Hue. Some of Diem's earliest American supporters were Catholic members of the U.S. Congress, including Mike Mansfield. The Catholic Church contributed substantially to Vietnamese charities. Archbishop Francis Spellman came to Vietnam several times during my tenure in Saigon. He was very supportive not only of Diem but of the whole effort in South Vietnam. I deny, however, that Diem's government was a "Roman Catholic dictatorship," an accusation that appeared frequently in the American press. At the time of the Buddhist crisis, four of the seventeen cabinet ministers were Christians. Most of the others were Buddhists. Nguyen Thuan described himself to me as "a confused Confucian!"

No government in Vietnam could have been representative of the people in the same sense as in a democracy where people are used to self-government, but the Vietnamese people did not regard the South Vietnamese government as Roman Catholic. It certainly was not Catholic in the sense of being unrepresentative on religious grounds. As a political leader, Diem was not a creature of religion. He was a nationalist and a dedicated anti-Communist, but certainly not a religious bigot. He did not, for example, do anything that I know of to promote the hierarchy of his brother, Archbishop Thuc, who had been in the Catholic ministry for a long time and who received his promotions from the Vatican, not Diem.

I had many opportunities—on trips into the provinces, in visits to pagodas, in long philosophical conversations—to explore in depth Diem's beliefs and attitudes toward religion. Never did I detect on his part disapproval, much less contempt, of the Buddhist faith. It is true that the Christians of South Vietnam, many of whom were Roman Catholic refugees from the North, were more actively anti–Viet Cong than the Buddhists. It is true that Diem considered his main purpose as a leader to be to rally his countrymen to resist Viet Cong aggression. But it is definitely not true that Diem disdained Buddhism. On the contrary, he went out of his way to support and encourage Buddhist schools and pagodas by putting scarce government funds into them, and, in particular, by making personal visits to the bonzes in remote provinces. His attitude and actions reflected respect for their religion and tolerance toward others in religious matters.

There was, true enough, a tendency of ambitious people in the government, both civilian and military, to convert to Roman Catholicism because they thought it would help advance their careers. On one occasion, long before the incident in Hue, I was in President Diem's office when a message was brought to him that a certain ARVN officer was "bucking" for promotion. The message included the information that the officer had recently converted to the Roman Catholic faith. Diem hit the ceiling. "If men like this would do their jobs," he said, "they would win promotions—but not by trying to curry favor with this government by changing religions!" I knew the President well enough to judge that his reaction was sincere.

Although I believed that there was no religious persecution in South Vietnam, I had no doubts about the seriousness of the May 8 incident in Hue. Such occurrences could trigger long-lasting repercussions. My family and I were scheduled to leave Saigon on May 9 for a vacation on a sailboat in the Aegean. Our two older daughters were already in Greece awaiting our arrival, but my wife, two younger daughters, and I postponed our departure in case the situation deteriorated. We stayed in Saigon for two relatively calm weeks. The government's report on the incident was issued during this period. While the report failed to establish culpability for the eight deaths, it seemed objective, accurate, and fair. Finally, I decided that the immediate crisis had passed and that we could leave for our vacation with a clear conscience.

My wife was uncomfortable with the decision. Too many persistent questions from Vietnamese friends about exactly when we were leaving had made her uneasy, and she suggested that we not go at all. But the plans were made, our daughters were waiting for us, and the State Department had issued our travel orders, so I convinced her that it was safe to go. Both my deputy at the mission, Bill Trueheart, and the State Department in Washington had our daily schedule. It was understood that Trueheart would contact me in an emergency through the U.S. Embassy in Athens, or elsewhere en route. The atmosphere appeared relatively calm in both Saigon and the provinces, and we left Saigon on May 23, 1963, to join our daughters in Greece.

I could not have made a worse mistake. I left my post on the eve of the storm—a storm that eventually destroyed nine years of constructive American help and support for South Vietnam's independence.

8

The Buddhist Crisis

We flew from Saigon to New Delhi on May 23 and spent the night at the beautiful residence of the U.S. Ambassador to India. The Galbraiths had invited us, but because of our delay they were away, so we enjoyed their hospitality all by ourselves. The next day we visited the Taj Mahal, then we were off to Cairo for a two-day trip up the Nile to Luxor and its surrounding ancient Egyptian tombs. In Athens we joined our two elder daughters. It was a joyful reunion. There were no messages about Vietnam at the Embassy, and the next day we set sail from Piraeus on a rented *kaike*, a Greek fishing boat rigged to sleep six. It had sails and an inboard motor—a sturdy little craft. That was fortunate, for on the second day rough weather set in. A *melteme* blew steadily from the north for eight days, causing the Aegean to kick up in unexpected high waves. We had our hands full, but the islands we visited offered safe harbors and fascinating sights.

During this ten-day sailing vacation, I called several times from small Aegean islands to the U.S. Embassy and the CIA station chief in Athens to check for messages from Saigon and Washington. Each time I was told there were none. One of these calls was prompted by a picture we saw in a small Greek newspaper on the island of Mykonos. It was Malcolm Browne's photo of Tich Quang Duc's suicide. There were no details, and I mistakenly relied on the assurances I had received that I would be notified if any unusual disturbances occurred in Vietnam. That proved to be a cardinal error on my part.

The State Department had arranged for us to return by ship from Genoa to New York City. I was scheduled to give two speeches on Vietnam in New York and then go to Washington for consultations. On the voyage from Genoa to New York, there was little news about Vietnam on the ship's radio bulletin, but we did hear that Henry Cabot Lodge had been appointed to succeed me as Ambassador to Vietnam. This was the first I heard of Lodge's appointment.

When we arrived in New York, I found a personal letter from my deputy, Bill Trueheart, waiting for me. The letter was brief and gave few details. It said that a major crisis had developed in Vietnam about two weeks after our departure, arising from the incident at Hue on May 8, and that relations between our two governments had deteriorated badly. Trueheart added that he had been unable to let me know because events had been so fast-moving that he could not accurately describe the situation. His letter included a message from Minister Thuan saying, "President Diem asks you to return as soon as possible." A separate message from Roger Hilsman also waited for me, asking me to come to Washington immediately.

I received Trueheart's letter a few hours before speaking at the New York Council on Foreign Relations. The audience there was better informed on recent events in Vietnam than I was. I could only admit this, and my report on how things had previously been improving was politely received, but unconvincing. Then I flew to Washington.

The atmosphere in Washington differed vastly from my last visit in January 1962, and from that of the Honolulu meetings in May. There was great agitation and confusion. Some differences of opinion were evident, but, clearly, serious opposition had developed to what had been viewed as a successful policy in Vietnam. The euphoria of a few weeks before had vanished. Reconstructing events from telegrams and reports I saw in the State Department, the crisis developed as follows.

A large group of militant Buddhists, led by an organization called the General Association of Vietnamese Buddhists, had demanded reparations and apologies from the South Vietnamese government on account of the incident at Hue on May 8. The government refused, the Buddhists charged religious persecution, and tensions built up. Then, on June 11, 1963, an elderly, re- spected Buddhist monk ceremoniously burned himself to death in the middle of downtown Saigon. Some members of the American press, who had been alerted that something dramatic was about to happen, were present at Tich Quang Duc's death. Words and pictures recorded the gruesome scene. Mal- colm Browne's photograph of the old man sitting motionless in the midst of flames shocked the world. American public opinion turned firmly against President Diem.[10]

In Vietnam the Buddhist radicals continued their agitation, fueling the theme of religious persecution. Diem and Nhu remained obdurate, and more bonzes killed themselves. The whole machinery of cooperation between the American mission and the South Vietnamese government nearly collapsed. It was a fast-moving picture, as Trueheart had written, but who was to blame? The exchanges of messages between Washington and Saigon during my ab- sence showed that Trueheart carried out his instructions with a vengeance— demanding that the Diem government reach a settlement with the Buddhists, without conditions or a thorough evaluation of the merits of the case or the motives of the agitators.

It is still incomprehensible to me that my deputy in Saigon and my colleagues in the State Department allowed this crisis in U.S.-GVN relations to develop without letting me know what was happening. They had our daily schedule. I had their assurances. Upon timely notification, I could have returned within twenty-four hours, and I believe I could have helped to prevent the tragedies that followed.[11]

In Washington I met with Hilsman and Harriman and once with President Kennedy. I believe Secretary Rusk was away. In any case, I do not recall having a talk with him then. Harriman was testy and uncommunicative. He appeared not to want me to return to Saigon. I suspect that I had not been notified during my vacation because the anti-Diem forces in Washington had not wanted me to return to Vietnam. Seeing in this crisis a chance for a fresh start, they may have wanted it to come to a head, to make a change in government in Saigon inevitable. Throughout this period, Trueheart acted on strict orders from Washington, as the records subsequently revealed. In talks with Harriman and Hilsman, I said frankly what I thought about the way this crisis was being handled, including the evident lack of consultation and proper coordination in Washington. I asked to return to Saigon immediately.

President Kennedy and I had a brief meeting, and I recall that his manner was more calm and cordial than what I had encountered in the State Department. It was he who agreed that I should return as promptly as possible to Saigon, telling me to do my best to help restore confidence and trust until Lodge arrived. I do not remember any big cheers from the State Department on this decision.

I returned to Saigon on June 10, 1963. Reporters would be present at the airport, and I knew I would have to make a statement upon my arrival. On the flight I had considered carefully what I would say, knowing that tensions were high on both sides. I spoke of the strong American tradition of religious toleration and the vital importance of this concept to our relationship with South Vietnam. I said this in an even-handed way, without accusing the Diem government of religious intolerance, and spoke of the urgent need for further negotiations and good-faith agreements with the Buddhist leaders. My remarks were reported in full to Washington and, surprisingly, the State Department sent me a word of confirmation and congratulations.

As soon as I got to our house from the airport, I received a call from President Diem asking me to come to see him. When I arrived, I found him cordial but deeply troubled. He had read my remarks at the airport and said, "I wish we could do this. That would be great. But it's not up to us, it's up to the other side. We can't negotiate ourselves out of existence." Diem's government, I learned, had been negotiating with the Buddhists for several weeks. Nguyen Thuan, who had urged Diem to reach a compromise based on Bui Van Luong's investigation of the Hue incident, joined Luong on the negotiating committee, together with Vice President Tho. They met with four older respected Buddhist leaders and in early July came up with what seemed to be a satisfactory agreement. The agreement reaffirmed the principle of religious freedom and the Buddhists' right to fly their flag and noted that the government would continue to contribute to the pagodas. It contained a statement, which Diem said was unnecessary, that there would be no religious discrimination or persecution. It did not offer reparations for the Hue incident.

Vice President Tho, Luong, and Thuan took the proposed settlement back to the South Vietnamese government, and the Buddhist representatives to their fellow bonzes. The radical General Association of Vietnamese Buddhists, led by Thich Tri Quang, quickly struck it down. This sequence was repeated both before and after my return. Several times Thuan told me that the Buddhist and government representatives thought they had reached an agreement. Each time Tri Quang denounced it. His faction's demands became more and more extreme, until finally it was calling for the government to concede to its own downfall. The negotiations had reached an impasse.

On the government's side, Counselor and Madame Nhu urged Diem not to compromise further. Meanwhile, the American press gave the crisis sensational coverage. Most of the journalists interpreted it as a genuine revolt against religious persecution, dwelling on the theme of a "Roman Catholic dictatorship." David Halberstam, the *New York Times* representative, said later that he always regarded the crisis as a political, not a religious, uprising. That may be true, but I ask any fair-minded person to recall his reports from Saigon and judge whether that crucial point came through in his dispatches. The South Vietnamese government, never adept at dealing with dissent or the American media, certainly mishandled the Buddhist crisis. But so did the U.S. government. Thuan told me later that he tried twice during our vacation to get our Embassy to send me a telegram from Diem saying, "Please come back and help us mediate this crisis." Trueheart said that he would notify me but never did until it was too late. Washington, spurred into action by the American press, sent hotheaded instructions to Saigon. The only people who handled the situation skillfully were the Buddhist militants.

I believe the Buddhist crisis could have been resolved had Washington not begun to hammer on the table, demanding impossible concessions from the Vietnamese government. If the United States had endeavored to persuade and not to order Diem to be more flexible in the early stages of the crisis before Thich Tri Quang took over, I believe the negotiations would have succeeded. Instead, valuable time was lost, and the Buddhist dissident movement came into the hands of individuals who had only one objective: to overthrow the South Vietnamese government.

At the time, I could see a parallel between the objectives of the Buddhist agitators and those of the Viet Cong, but we had no concrete evidence that the uprising was a Viet Cong plot. Obviously our government did not believe that it was, because a few weeks later Henry Cabot Lodge gave Thich Tri Quang, whom President Nguyen Van Thieu later branded a Communist agent, asylum in the U.S. Embassy. I believe now, however, that the crisis was a Viet Cong conspiracy.

The mission had evidence that some of the Buddhist agitators had only recently come into the pagodas. They had simply shaved their heads, donned saffron robes, and become bonzes (monks). One could suspect that they were no more bonzes than I was. Few Vietnamese had heard of the General Association of Vietnamese Buddhists, the central organization of the agitators, until a few years before the crisis. There had not been a formal hierarchy before. Bonzes in the provinces ran their own pagodas as independent entities, performing their own funerals, weddings, and so forth. When I returned from our ill-fated vacation, I found on my desk numerous letters from Buddhist bonzes in the provinces, some of whom I had met, saying that they were not part of the General Association of Vietnamese Buddhists. They had no connection with its leaders, had had nothing to do with it, and did not subscribe to its antigovernment policy or its political goals. Those letters may still be in the files from Saigon. I had no time to answer them.

Much of the antigovernment propaganda was in English. We lived near the Xa Loi Pagoda, and my normal route to the office passed it. Frequently, banners proclaiming, in English, "Down with the government" and "Destroy the government" were stretched all the way across the street. Why were they written in English? Most of the Vietnamese passing by could not read them. This does not necessarily prove a Communist connection, but it proves the agitators' skill in manipulating the American media. Certainly, it had a Viet Cong smell to it.

A Vietnamese acquaintance related to me the background of Tich Quang Duc's self-immolation, that horrible event which started the public hysteria. Dr. Young, a Vietnamese physician, treated President Diem for bursitis (I have changed his name for security reasons). He also regularly attended Tich Quang Duc in the Xa Loi Pagoda. He told me that he had reported to President Diem his suspicions about things he had observed at the pagoda. Several new monks at the pagoda, all young activists, were trying to convince the Venerable Quang Duc to kill himself. Some years earlier, Quang Duc had made a suicide pact with a Buddhist monk in Hanoi, who later took his own life. Quang Duc was contemplating suicide to redeem his pledge, a practice not unprecedented among Vietnamese Buddhists. The elderly bonze Quang Duc was not concerned with politics, nor was he known to be against the Diem government, but the new monks were prevailing upon him to sacrifice himself.

His physician told me that upon hearing this, Diem said, "This sounds ominous," and asked, "What can we do about it?" Dr. Young replied that his mother was an old friend of Quang Duc's, having attended school with him. He volunteered to ask her to talk to him. She did and reported to her son that the old monk had confirmed that the new bonzes were encouraging him to kill himself, but that she had talked him out of it. Dr. Young in turn related this to President Diem. Tragically, his mother was mistaken. Dr. Young and his mother were convinced that the new monks were either Communists themselves, or Communist sympathizers. If his story is true, then political agitators used Tich Quang Duc in a sinister and frightful way as the tool of a vicious political plot, which misled the American press and the U.S. government into the gravest political error, and eventually into war.

Whether the activists were directly linked to the Viet Cong or not, I believe the Buddhist crisis was basically a very clever ploy that used a religious mask and a great many naive people. A political plot to overthrow the South Vietnamese government, it was also aimed through publicity at the United States and U.S. support of the Diem government. It came out exactly as the activists intended. Our media and our government were incredibly gullible.

When I returned to Vietnam in July 1963, Saigon was in an uproar. Buddhist agitators demonstrated in front of our home, and frequently demonstrators blocked the street in front of the Xa Loi Pagoda so that we had to detour to get to the Embassy office. The atmosphere at our mission mirrored the turmoil outside it. Several of my colleagues told me, "You should never have left." Things have really gone to pieces. Trueheart has been pounding the table with Diem and has gotten relations to a pass where it is impossible to deal with the government." General Harkins put it in a nutshell: "It looks like the State Department thinks Diem is the enemy, rather than the Viet Cong."

I had a very straight talk with Trueheart, who reiterated *mea culpa* regarding his failure to keep me informed. On his change of position, he said, "I'm afraid you have another Joe Mendenhall on your hands." A few others had, like him, shifted with the changing winds from Washington, but most of the key people—certainly the military side, the CIA under John Richardson, the USOM under Joseph Brent, and most of the political section under Mel Manfull—had grave misgivings as to where we were headed. They wanted, if possible, to put things back on track so that they could work constructively with their opposite numbers in the Vietnamese government. South Vietnamese officials with whom we had worked for months or years were giving their Embassy counterparts the brushoff, not returning their telephone calls and things of that sort. Many mission employees had garbage thrown in their yards, by Nhu's men, they believed. Relations between the mission and the Diem government were at a standoff.

Our first job was to reestablish communications, which I tried to do immediately by going to see President Diem. I told him that the mission wanted to return to the kind of working relationship we had had with his government until June. He replied that he would like that too, but he felt that Washington was changing its policy very fast and that the United States was using its leverage of aid to undermine his government. He was very resentful of this. Diem seemed surprised when I mentioned the garbage being thrown in our people's yards. "Look," I told him, "this is child's play. What's going on here?" He responded, sincerely I think, that he had not known about it. The incidents ceased soon thereafter.

Six weeks of strenuous efforts to get things back on track followed. We were overwhelmingly busy, trying to pick up the pieces of U.S.–Vietnamese cooperation. Early in this period, President Diem asked me if the impending change of ambassadors denoted a change in American policy. I assured him that it did not. I had been told in Washington that no such change would occur. Noting that he had information to the contrary, Diem asked me to present the question formally to my government. Accordingly, I cabled his inquiry to Washington and received in response a telegram from "Highest Authority," a code phrase for President Kennedy, stating that there was no intention of changing our policy. I took this telegram to President Diem, translating it for him in his office. He shook his head sadly. "I believe you," he said, "but I don't believe the message you have received."

It was about this time that we received reports that Ngo Dinh Nhu was planning to take control of the government from his brother. Nhu had allegedly met with a number of leading South Vietnamese generals and suggested to them that he was dubious about some of the things President Diem was doing and that he might have to cut his ties to his brother and perhaps establish his own leadership. The U.S. mission's consensus about this report was that Nhu was testing the generals' loyalty, trying to draw out the dissenters. Rumors of a "Nhu coup," or that he intended to sell out to the Viet Cong, proliferated. I think they were part of the tumult that grew out of the Buddhist crisis, and untrue.

We had been aware for some time that Nhu had been meeting with Viet Cong leaders. In the spring of 1963, I had gone to see him in his office to protest one of his wife's unfortunate speeches and to enlist his help in preventing them. He received me pleasantly. After I sat down, he asked, "Do you know who just left that chair?" I said I did not, and he named a prominent Viet Cong leader. I inquired what the man had been doing there. Nhu answered that he came at his invitation, that the government was trying to bring this Viet Cong officer and his units to the side of the Republic of Vietnam. He added that he met frequently with high Viet Cong cadres and that President Diem knew about these meetings. The Viet Cong leaders came to Nhu's office under a gentlemen's agreement that they would not be arrested while they were there.

The South Vietnamese government had announced in April 1963 a policy of "Chieu Hoi," or "Open Arms," a formal program to encourage Viet Cong defections. The revelation that Communist leaders were coming to the Palace surprised me, but it fit into Nhu's ideas about attracting Viet Cong political leaders and military cadres away from the rebellion and into a broadened government, which Diem would head. Nhu felt strongly that such a development was possible. These meetings with Viet Cong cadres also may have included discussions of the ground rules, as it were, for the military struggle. The participants may have exchanged comments like "We'll prevent further American intervention if you keep the Chinese out of this affair." But the primary purpose of Nhu's meetings with the Viet Cong was to induce defections.

Washington reacted negatively to our reports about these meetings. Some people felt that Nhu's actions came close to a betrayal of the United States and were none too pleased when I suggested that perhaps this was a way to compose things. "Give them a chance," I suggested. "The South Vietnamese leaders are not stupid, and they are not going to risk their necks or betray us." Washington, especially the State Department, mistrusted Nhu in particular. Nhu was, indeed, a complicated person, but I am convinced that he was loyal to his brother—as his brother was to him.

Just before the end of my tenure in Vietnam, I received urgent instructions to get President Diem to make a public statement of reconciliation with the Buddhists. Diem hesitated, not, he explained, because he had reservations about reconciliation, but because he doubted gravely the utility of such a statement. He maintained that he had done his utmost already. I encouraged him to make another conciliatory gesture and finally arranged for Maggie Higgins, a journalist and a trusted Diem supporter, to interview him. Higgins got a statement from President Diem, which she published. "My policy of nondiscrimination on religious grounds is irreversible," he told her in his characterisitically convoluted way.

Getting this statement, which the State Department had demanded for reasons of public relations, was not easy. I had to do it through a third party, because by that time Diem was not going to make such a statement directly to the U.S. government. Even so, the mutual respect and personal confidence we shared endured until I left Saigon. In fact, during my last weeks there, I had more influence with Diem than with my own government. Little by little, our mission had restored relations with the South Vietnamese government, despite the American press and TV. Thanks to General Harkins, John Richardson, and others, things had calmed down, and some reconciliation occurred. People in the mission and the government could once again talk to each other. But the atmosphere was changed. The trust we had so carefully constructed over two and a half years was not to be revived.

I requested permission to remain in Vietnam until we could reinforce this tenuous relationship. But Washington denied my request and ordered me to leave before Ambassador Lodge got there. My wife and I left Saigon for the last time on August 15, 1963. During my farewell call on President Diem, we again discussed whether my departure signaled a change in policy. I left knowing that I had not convinced him that American policy would remain the same. I do not, however, think that Diem anticipated immediate problems with Lodge. His questions focused on policy, not on the individual implementing it.

As my family and I were leaving for the Saigon airport on August 15, 1963, after many farewells, we were handed a copy of the *Times of Viet Nam*, a progovernment daily published in English by two Americans, Anne and Gene Gregory, longtime residents of Saigon. It contained the following editorial about our departure and Ambassador Lodge's arrival:

Big Shoes to Fill

The first American Ambassador to Vietnam really worthy of being addressed by his title is being recalled from Vietnam.

The Nolting era in Vietnam has been one marked by the kind of friendship capable of sustaining differences of opinion and direct attack of the Viet Cong propaganda machine, but apparently the criticism and ridicule of the American press was too much.

For the past eight months the American press has apparently been out to "get Nolting." Their antipathy for President Ngo Dinh Diem, his family and his government is nothing new, and it has rubbed off heavily on Ambassador Nolting. He has been attacked and offended constantly and consistently by the American press.

The why of this treatment is not a pretty story. The Ambassador has exhibited the courage to do his job without pandering to *any* press. In return they discredit his considered evaluations of the situation in Vietnam. They scorn him because he does not try to "run the show" as a good imperialist should.

And now the "Buddhist leaders" are profiting from the image of Nolting projected abroad by the press to attack him for an honest, reasoned, intelligent statement, attacking him with an insidious and not so subtle appeal for "good" Americans to identify themselves in opposition to Nolting. This would, of course, serve well the interests of those toting neutralism as the "solution to the Vietnam problem", which is exactly what the Viet Cong want.

But in Free Vietnam Nolting will be remembered as the symbol of [an] era when, nation to nation, the United States and Viet Nam found the basis of understanding which resulted in a workable collaboration for the national interests of both countries and the interests of the Free World. Ambassador Nolting somehow seemed intuitively to know how to represent in its Sunday best the greatest power of the free world in this newly independent nation while always showing the due respect for Vietnam's national integrity.

When the Strategic Hamlets are completed, when the Viet Cong menace has waned to a policing problem, when the Open Arms returnees are all settled in hamlets—when victory has arrived—many Vietnamese will remember, with no injury to national pride, that the help for the beginning of all the programs that spelled success came to Vietnam when Nolting, the American Ambassador who understood the people and the problems of Vietnam and the role of his own nation, was here.

Most Vietnamese are surely flattered that such a prominent personality as Henry Cabot Lodge is to represent the United States in Vietnam, but he has mighty big shoes to fill.

The *Times of Viet Nam* was regarded by many Vietnamese and some Americans, including me, as being extravagantly progovernment. After the coup, its presses were smashed by the anti-Diem mobs in Saigon. It did, however, serve as an antidote to the vicious and unfounded attacks of other newspapers, local and foreign. I was embarrassed by the editorial, especially by its references to my predecessors, but was encouraged by its welcome to my successor, Ambassador Lodge.

The group of journalists at the airport, of course, wanted a farewell statement. "What was your reaction to the *Times* editorial?" someone asked. I said I thought that it was overstated. "Do you think the press was instrumental in your removal?" "No," I replied (untruthfully), "I was simply dis-Lodged. I wish this country, our many friends here and my successor the greatest possible success."

On our way back to Washington we stopped in Honolulu, where, on August 20 and 21, I met with Ambassador Lodge, Hilsman, Admiral Felt, and Paul Kattenburg, the new chairman of the Vietnam Task Force in the State Department. We discussed with Lodge his new assignment, in detail. Lodge gave me the definite impression that he thought good working relations with the Vietnamese government should and could be restored, and assured me there would be no change on his part in U.S. policy. It was during the second day of these meetings that we learned of the crackdown on the pagodas.

At approximately 12:30 A.M., August 21, Vietnamese police and special forces began raiding several pagodas in Saigon, Hue, and other towns. They arrested over 1,000 persons. That same day, President Diem declared a "state of siege" and placed South Vietnam under martial law. The government announced that it was "strongly determined not to tolerate the exploitation of religion for political purposes." Although the Vietnamese armed forces enforced martial law, it was later established that Nhu's special forces had carried out the attacks on the pagodas without the knowledge or aid of the regular army. President Diem may not have known about the raids beforehand, but he failed to denounce them after they happened.

In Washington, the State Department issued the following statement:

On the basis of information from Saigon, it appears that the Government of the Republic of Viet-Nam has instituted serious repressive measures against Vietnamese Buddhist leaders. The action represents a direct violation by the Vietnamese Government of assurances that it was pursuing a policy of reconciliation with the Buddhists. The United States deplores repressive actions of this nature.

The news stunned us equally in Hawaii. We were amazed and angered that it came on the heels of Diem's statement of his policy of conciliation. I was shocked and immediately sent President Diem a personal telegram: "This is the first time that you've ever gone back on your word to me." Now I regret sending that telegram. Later I saw Nguyen Dinh Thuan in Paris and asked him if he recalled it. He answered, "Yes, I took it to the President. The President read it, shook his head and said, 'He doesn't know what the provocation was.'" The "provocation" was, in fact, continued packing of arms in the Xa Loi and other pagodas, continued riots clamoring for the government's overthrow, and a total unwillingness on the part of Thich Tri Quang and his militants to compromise on anything. When I returned to Washington, I would plunge immediately into a controversy over what to do about the Diem government, but by that time it was too late. As Roger Hilsman put it in his book *To Move a Nation*, "After August 21, the facts became irrelevant."

9

Washington: Vacillation and Betrayal

From the meetings with Lodge in Honolulu, I returned to Washington on August 26, 1963, having spent the previous weekend in Virginia with my family. There I found a letter from President Kennedy:

THE WHITE HOUSE

WASHINGTON

August 15, 1963

Dear Mr. Ambassador:

It is with regret that I accept your resignation upon a date to be determined.

I want to express my personal appreciation for the outstanding manner in which you have represented the United States as Ambassador to Viet-Nam for the past two and one half years. In carrying out your mission, you have served your country with a high sense of dedication and purpose in a most demanding position.

You have made a significant contribution to strengthening relations between the Governments and peoples of the United States and Viet-Nam, and your actions have embodied the determination of the United States and other free nations to assist Viet-Nam in maintaining its freedom.

You have my deep gratitude and best wishes for continued success.

Sincerely yours,

(Signed)

John F. Kennedy

The Honorable Frederick E. Nolting, Jr.
American Ambassador
Saigon

This was the kind of routine letter most ambassadors receive upon recall or transfer. I was pleased to get it, but it had a special consequence. Almost immediately, I got a call from the White House. A public relations staff member asked me to give the letter no publicity. I said that I had no intention of doing so. "That's fine," he said. "The President would find it awkward and embarrassing because of his references to the close relations you established between the Government of South Vietnam and the United States." A few minutes later, I stood in Roger Hilsman's office at the State Department and read a copy of a telegram that had been sent to Ambassador Lodge on August 24, and I understood all too well the changes that had occurred in the relations between South Vietnam and the United States in so short a time. A plot had been launched to overthrow the constitutional government of President Diem, and President Kennedy was aware of it, if not entirely sympathetic. Naturally, he did not want to be caught in the contradiction between his former policy and the emerging one. I have said nothing about Kennedy's letter, except to my wife, until now.

The telegram of August 24 turned out to be a decisive factor in leading our country into the longest and most unnecessary war in American history. The message has been widely discussed and interpreted. Briefly, its origin is as follows.

Several South Vietnamese generals had secretly approached a member of the U.S. mission in Saigon to ask how the United States would react to a military takeover of the government. Ambassador Lodge, who had been there only two days, cabled the inquiry to Washington. It reached the State Department on Saturday, August 24, when several key policymakers were out of town. Harriman and Hilsman were there and reacted immediately. They composed a telegram instructing Lodge to give Diem the option of removing Nhu from his position as Counselor. If Diem refused, Lodge was to tell the generals secretly that the United States would cease to support Diem and would give them "direct support in any interim period of breakdown of central government mechanism." They had then cleared this text over the telephone with representatives of State (George Ball was acting Secretary because Rusk was away), Defense, CIA, and the White House staff. The President was consulted. Each person, including President Kennedy, who was vacationing on Cape Cod, had approved the telegram under the impression that other top officials had agreed with it. There was no formal meeting to discuss or coordinate the message.

Its wording was ambiguous, but the telegram's import was clear. The United States would support a change of government—a coup in South Vietnam—if Diem did not get rid of his brother, Nhu. While reading this message, I received a call from Bob McNamara. He too had been out of town when the telegram was "cleared." "Have you seen what's happened?" he asked.

"Yes," I replied, "I have just seen the telegram to Lodge." "I'm trying to get a meeting with the President on this," he said. "Will you come?" "You bet I will," I answered, "if I get invited." Soon thereafter, General Chester V. "Ted" Clifton, President Kennedy's military aide, notified me that the President wanted me to attend.

The meeting turned out to be a kind of National Security Council special group meeting, chaired by President Kennedy, who appeared harassed and worried. He said that he wanted to get "all sides of this picture."

Sharp disagreement over whether the telegram to Lodge had been properly coordinated, wise, or justified marked the meeting. Several of us felt that it had been extremely unwise and a disastrous mistake. Others argued that it would be almost impossible to call back the message. It was assumed that Lodge had already given the generals the signal and that the South Vietnamese government probably knew it. No one expected President Diem to knuckle under to the demand to dismiss his brother. Thus, it was argued, the new Ambassador could not now restore confidence between the Diem government and the United States no matter what he did or wanted to do.

It was a difficult situation for President Kennedy, who seemed especially upset by the lack of coordination in his government. Some of us tried to convince him to retreat from the consequences of the message. I am not sure he really wanted to, although at times he gave me the impression that he would like to get back on the old track if he could find a way. In any case, at the close of this meeting, the "green light" for a coup remained unchanged.

During the next couple of weeks, I attended several meetings on Vietnam. At the President's request, I expressed my own convictions, independently of those held by my superiors in the State Department. I felt too strongly to do otherwise. The basic issue was whether the U.S. government should connive to overthrow the Diem government. I argued that it should not. A coup would create a political vacuum, encourage the Communists, and wipe out the nine years of relatively successful support we had given South Vietnam— without the use of American combat forces. Furthermore, in supporting a coup, the United States would be doing exactly what President Kennedy had promised President Diem we would not do, namely, interfering in South Vietnam's internal affairs. Our moral commitment, the integrity of the United States, was at stake. Finally, I argued that the generals would be ineffective leaders. They would not gain the support of the South Vietnamese people and would naturally turn to the United States for more and more military help, including, probably, U.S. combat forces. I was appalled that our government would encourage a group of dissident generals to overthrow their elected government. It was wrong in principle and would, even if successfully executed, have disastrous long-range consequences for the United States as well as for Vietnam.

There had always been coup rumors in Vietnam. Hardly a week had passed during my time there when the mission did not get word, directly or indirectly, that a civilian or military person thought he would make a better leader than President Diem and could organize a better resistance to the Viet Cong if we would support him in a coup. An ARVN general might approach a U.S. military man, a Bao Dai adherent might speak to an Embassy political officer, someone else might contact a CIA officer, directly or indirectly. We routinely reported these overtures to Washington. Once General Tran Van Don and his brother-in-law, General Tran Thiem Kim, dined at our house. After dinner, as they sat on the sofa, they lit into President Diem. He was, they charged, unworthy to be President of the country. He was incapable of running South Vietnam; he interfered too much in military affairs; he was a bad political leader. He should be overthrown.

"Gentlemen," I responded, "you are my guests and I am an accredited diplomat to your government, which is headed by your President, who was elected. You have a chance to run for President. Don't give me this stuff about revolt and supporting a revolt. Why don't you do your duty as military men? The United States is not going to get into the question of a coup d'état." Their outburst had shocked me, but this was actually our stock answer to such comments. Whenever someone approached a mission employee about the possibility of a coup, the employee was to respond that the United States was not in the business of making or breaking the Vietnamese government. This was the responsibility of the Vietnamese people themselves through a legitimate process of elections held under their constitution at regular intervals. We were there to support the independence of South Vietnam through the government of its own choice, and, therefore, we would have nothing to do with any plotting. This had been the Ambassador's and the mission's response throughout the nine years of our diplomatic relations with South Vietnam. It remained the standard U.S. response to coup overtures until August 24, 1963.

Why this sudden change in policy? I put the question bluntly to Dean Rusk, who responded laconically, "We cannot stand any more burnings." "Do you really think," I said, "that the government of South Vietnam is responsible for these burnings?" In effect, he replied that it did not make any difference, that public opinion was overwhelming. No doubt some people in Washington, led by Harriman, actually thought a coup would be a quick way to bring the Vietnam struggle to a successful conclusion. They were fed up with Diem; they were tired of criticism by the media, which rose to a crescendo during the Buddhist crisis; they were impatient with the slow progress of pacification; *and* the 1964 presidential election was approaching.

At a meeting at the State Department chaired by Secretary Rusk, Harlan

Cleveland, then Assistant Secretary of State for International Organization Affairs, spoke at length about "world opinion." The thrust of his argument was that world opinion as reflected in the United Nations was strongly against the Diem government because of its "persecution" of Buddhists. Therefore the United States should not support that government. Who made that world opinion, I asked. How valid was it? Were the allegations true or false? Was the Diem government really to blame? These questions were brushed aside as irrelevant. Thus "world opinion" joined American "public opinion" in overwhelming any sense of fairness or fidelity toward an ally.

Vice President Lyndon Johnson was present at this meeting in the State Department. He listened to the arguments and then made one remark. Otto Passman, he observed, has been a "pain in the neck" to the Democrats in Congress for many years. (Passman was a Democratic Representative from Louisiana.) But do we try to throw him out? Do we try to undermine him with his own constituents? No, we try to get along with him as best we can. We should do the same with President Diem, he said. While not exactly the kind of remark I had hoped for, the comment was like a breath of fresh air in that meeting. Another time, at an NSC meeting with the President, Johnson told me privately, "Keep it up. You're gaining ground." I asked him if he would voice his views at the meeting: "We could stand some help, Mr. Vice President." He replied that the President had asked him to come to those meetings only to listen.

At the White House meetings I attended, President Kennedy seemed doubtful of the wisdom of a coup, but unsure as to what he could do. He had two powerful politicians to deal with, Harriman and Lodge. Both seemed determined to bring Diem to his knees. The young President cannot have relished his position. He called on many people for their opinions.

Harriman claimed that his purpose was not to destroy Diem, but to get rid of Nhu, and by various pressures to force reforms on the Vietnamese government. The exact nature of these reforms was never spelled out, except vaguely as making the government more democratic. Harriman, Hilsman, Under Secretary of State George Ball, and others argued that the Diem government had lost the support of the South Vietnamese people and was therefore incapable of winning against the Communists. They also claimed that the morale of the ARVN was affected by the Buddhist-inspired riots.

Most of the military and CIA representatives present disputed the latter argument, saying that they saw no evidence of deteriorating morale in South Vietnam's military forces. McNamara initially opposed U.S. complicity in the plot, as did CIA Director John McCone and his deputy, Pat Carter. General Maxwell Taylor was definitely opposed. William Colby, head of the CIA's Far Eastern Division, and General Krulak, of the Joint Staff, also argued against it. In general, the CIA, Defense, and Joint Chiefs' point of view coincided with my own, while the State Department and the USIA pushed in the opposite direction. But, of course, the anti-Diem group had already prejudiced the case severely by sending Lodge the message on August 24. Lodge himself strongly favored a coup. His messages indicated that he was acting more like an American proconsul than an Ambassador.

At the State Department, Paul Kattenburg had succeeded Chalmers (Ben) Wood as head of the Vietnam Task Force in the summer of 1963. Kattenburg had previously served in the Embassy in Saigon and, like Joe Mendenhall, held a low opinion of President Diem. While I strongly disagreed with him concerning Diem's character and leadership, I must give credit to him for making a straightforward recommendation. Kattenburg said that our government should seriously consider an alternative to the positions in the present debate. That alternative would be to tell Diem frankly that the United States would no longer continue its aid to South Vietnam, thus backing out of all commitments by the Eisenhower and Kennedy administrations to that country and avoiding further interference in its internal affairs. While radical, that suggestion would have given President Diem, his government, and his people a chance to decide their own course of action. At the time, I was far from agreement with it, but the suggestion was at least more honorable than the course finally pursued.

People on all sides of the issue felt strongly about it. Emotion often prevailed over reason. Once, during a National Security Council meeting, Harriman shouted, "Shut up! We've heard you before!" President Kennedy intervened to say that he wanted to hear what I was saying. Harriman's rudeness did not surprise me. I had encountered it before in his office, on my first day back in Washington.

The last time I had seen Harriman before that was when he came to Saigon in 1961 to demand that President Diem sign the Laos accords. He had stayed with us and, despite our disagreements about the terms of the Laotian treaty, he was a courteous and pleasant house guest. My family and I enjoyed his company and his confidence. Now the change was personal and vindictive. Some incidents were so petty as to be almost laughable.

When I was present at a National Security Council or Special Group meeting on Vietnam, it was always at the President's invitation, never at the State Department's behest. Either Robert Kennedy or General Clifton would call to say that the President wanted me to attend a particular meeting. Once, after receiving an invitation on short notice, I tried to get a ride to the White House with Rusk and Harriman. Going down to the basement where the official cars were parked, I waited with the chauffeur, whom I knew from years before. When Rusk and Harriman arrived, Harriman said, "What are you doing here?" "I'm going to the White House meeting," I said, "if you'll give me a ride." "Well, nobody's asked you." Yes, I informed them, the President had. So they indicated the front seat and promptly put up the glass partition between the front and back seats. The only difference this made was that the chauffeur and I had a more pleasant conversation than I would have had otherwise.

Rusk was not personally antagonistic, but he certainly remained aloof during this period, both at the State Department and at the White House meetings. This disappointed me. As a career officer who had worked with him, I was delighted when President Kennedy named Dean Rusk Secretary of State. But during my tenure as Ambassador, he never set foot in Vietnam, nor did he attend any of the Honolulu conferences. I could never get him to focus on our problems while I was in Vietnam. Policy fell by default first to Bob McNamara in Defense and then to Averell Harriman. As late as August 1963, when I went to Rusk to talk about Vietnam, he told me, "Averell's handling this."

On August 31, the dissident generals told General Harkins that there would be no coup. Apparently, they had lost their nerve. Lodge informed Washington, commenting, "There is neither the will nor the organization among the generals to accomplish anything." The imminence of a coup had faded, but dividend counsels and indecision continued in Washington, while in Saigon the coup plotters sought more assurances from Ambassador Lodge and tried to line up more military support.

I had been assigned to the USIA promotion board and spent most of my time there—as far away from the debates on Vietnam as the State Department could get me. I was, however, asked by the White House to attend another NSC meeting on Vietnam in September 1963. My recollection is that President Kennedy was still seeking a way out—to avoid a coup if possible. The positions of his principal advisors were divided as before, with one exception. Secretary of Defense McNamara seemed to have switched sides in the debate, from anti-coup to pro-coup. I never discovered his reasons. According to George C. Herring, some,

such as Nolting, advocated a final attempt at reconciliation. The failure of the August coup made clear, they argued, that there was no real alternative to Diem. President Diem was unlikely to remove Nhu, even under the most severe American pressure, and cuts in aid would only hurt the war against the Viet Cong, antagonize the South Vietnamese people, and further destabilize the country. There was still a chance, they concluded, that if the United States repaired its relations with the government the war might be won.[12]

I think that it was after this meeting broke up, or perhaps after a later one, that General Clifton asked me to jot down for President Kennedy what I thought would be necessary to "get back on the track with Diem." I wrote down these points:

1. A public statement by the President that he wants to restore our former working relationship.
2. No more cuts in aid or threats involving the composition of Diem's government.
3. A concrete demonstration of our President's purpose—specifically, replacing Lodge and Harriman.

Clifton handed the piece of paper to the President, who glanced at it. As he left the room, Kennedy said, "You don't expect me to do that, do you?"

On September 2, President Kennedy stated in a televised interview with Walter Cronkite: "I don't think that unless a greater effort is made by the government of Vietnam to win popular support that the war can be won out there. . . . We are prepared to continue to assist them, but I don't think the war can be won unless the people support the effort and, in my opinion, in the last two months the government has gotten out of touch with the people." When Cronkite asked, "Do you think this government still has time to regain the support of the people?," Kennedy replied, "I do. With changes in policy and perhaps in personnel, I think it can. If it doesn't make those changes, I think the chances of winning it would not be very good." In October, the administration ceased shipments to Vietnam of rice, tobacco, and powdered milk under the commodity import program, and discontinued funds for Nhu's special forces. Why rice and powdered milk? I could understand that cutting off funds for Nhu's special forces had a specific thrust, but cutting off supplies of rice and milk would only weaken the economy and hurt the poor. Our USOM people in Vietnam had spent years educating the peasants to use powdered milk to help feed undernourished babies. Suddenly, the supply was cut off. It was yet another example of lack of coordination and common sense in Washington.

In Saigon, President Kennedy's statement on TV was interpreted as a signal for change in the South Vietnamese government. This impression deepened as Lodge kept himself aloof from Diem, waiting for U.S. pressures to work, and gave Thich Tri Quang asylum in the U.S. Embassy. Meanwhile, rumors of conflict over policy between the CIA and the Embassy—i.e., between John Richardson and Lodge—surfaced and were reported in both Saigon and Washington. Richardson favored continuing support for Diem, while Lodge advocated a change. Although there was no question of Richardson's having taken things into his own hands or having disobeyed instructions, Lodge, thinking of the CIA's connections with Nhu, questioned the wisdom of having the CIA Station Chief directly involved in operational matters. All of this was described in the press as part of a larger struggle over who would control the Embassy. Public reports applauded Lodge for having taken total charge of the mission and policy in Vietnam. Lodge won the applause of the anti-Diem media by the simple expedient of joining them in their anti-Diem crusade.

On October 4, 1963, John Richardson was called to Washington, reportedly for consultations. He left Saigon the next day. In a news conference four days later, President Kennedy stated, "I know that the transfer of Mr. John Richardson, who is a very dedicated public servant, has led to surmises. But I can just assure you flatly that the CIA has not carried out independent activities but has operated under close control of the Director of Central Intelligence, operating with the cooperation of the National Security Council and under my instructions." Richardson did not return to Vietnam. Despite President Kennedy's accurate assessment of his caliber as an officer, I felt that the administration had treated him shabbily.

Ambassador Lodge and his former friend, General Paul Harkins, also disagreed. In spite of the Buddhist-inspired riots in Saigon and Hue and the ambivalence of the Kennedy administration toward the Diem government, Harkins kept his eyes focused on the struggle in the countryside against the Viet Cong insurgents. His reading of the overall situation in Vietnam in the fall of 1963 was altogether different from that of Ambassador Lodge. Harkins reported that progress against the Viet Cong was continuing, that the Strategic Hamlets program was gaining strength, that the ARVN was not affected by the Buddhist agitation and the political turmoil in Saigon, and that good progress toward pacification and economic gains continued in most provinces.

Although never prone to make pronouncements on political matters, Paul Harkins told me, and later sent strong telegrams to Washington to the same effect, that he thought it was "crazy" for the United States to turn against President Diem. His view was shared by his Chief of Staff, Lieutenant General Weede, by his MAAG chief, Major General Timmes, and by most of our military advisors in Vietnam. Admiral Felt (CINCPAC), who was close to the situation, and the Joint Chiefs of Staff in Washington held similar views.

Ambassador Lodge went to Saigon with a different view—a *political* view. Contrary to what he had told me in Honolulu a week earlier, he seemed determined to bring President Diem to heel. After a short time, Lodge was not speaking to Harkins—or to Diem.

During the time we served together in Vietnam, Paul Harkins and I had discussed our mutual problems many times. One of them, of course, was the problem of leadership in South Vietnam—specifically President Diem. Both of us knew Diem's weaknesses and strengths. Both of us knew his critics in Vietnam's military hierarchy. We knew which of the generals had ambitions to succeed him. We knew something about these men's limited abilities, their rivalries, and their jealousies. Neither of us could discern a real leader among them.

General Duong Van Minh was something of a popular hero, having bravely resisted the Japanese in the forties. His official position was Chief of the General Staff of the Vietnamese Armed Forces, a post comparable in name to the U.S. Chairman of the Joint Chiefs of Staff, but he did little except complain about the inadequacies of the government he was paid to serve. Privately, Harkins and I called him "General Bellyache."

In the interval between the abortive coup plot inspired by the telegram of August 25 and the actual revolt on November 1, I had the opportunity to see, in some cases to participate in, the Kennedy administration's handling of this critical issue. In twenty-two years of public service, I never saw anything resembling the confusion, vacillation, and lack of coordination in the U.S. government. While I had sympathy for President Kennedy in his dilemma, one cannot admire his failure to take control. The Harriman-Lodge axis seemed too strong for him.

In Saigon, Lodge was doing everything possible within his loose and often conflicting instructions to encourage a revolution. In Washington, Harriman saw to it that the pressures against Diem—both moral pressures and physical sanctions—were not relaxed.

In the end, the American position came down to a disgraceful one: encouraging a coup while pretending we had nothing to do with it. As a result of Lodge's secret assurances to the dissident generals and U.S. sanctions against Diem, coup pressures continued to build in Vietnam, finally erupting on November 1, 1963.

I will skip the brave fight of the Palace Guards against overwhelming odds, except to note that Major General Nguyen Thieu, commander of ARVN's Fifth Division headquartered near Saigon, led the attack on the Palace.

When it was all over, a military junta headed by General Duong Van "Big" Minh took control of the government. Diem and Nhu were dead. The first radio reports from Saigon said they had committed suicide. In fact, they were murdered on Big Minh's orders in the back of an armored personnel carrier, shot in the back of the head with their hands tied.

My family and I heard the unfolding reports from Saigon with disbelief, then horror, then anger. Aside from personal reactions, I felt then, as I do now, that our country had betrayed an honest ally and that we would suffer the consequences in one way or another. Our deep concern for the future of South Vietnam and our many friends there, Vietnamese and American, was numbing.

There were relatively few people in Washington, in or out of government, who shared our feelings. The Colby family was among those who did. So were the John Richardsons. On a long-standing invitation of the Colbys, the six of us had dinner together that night. It was good to be with trustworthy friends on that tragic day.

Two days after the coup, Roger Hilsman called me at USIA to ask how the United States could save the Nhu children. Madame Nhu and her oldest daughter had been out of the country at the time of the coup, but her three youngest children were still in Vietnam, in hiding. I said, "Roger, if you really mean it, I would do this. Call Paul Harkins—*direct*, not through the Embassy. Ask him to try to find the children. If he can, ask him to send a U.S. chopper to pick them up. Be sure to have a reliable Vietnamese or French-speaking person aboard. The children may not want to come. Explain to them that their mother needs them. Fly them out of the country without stopping in Saigon, if Paul can do it." This was done, and the children were eventually reunited with their mother. Madame Nhu commented later that she expected them to be slaughtered. At least that needless tragedy was prevented.

I do not think that President Kennedy expected exactly the outcome that occurred on November 1 and 2. He was reported to have been shocked and horrified by news of the murders of the Ngo brothers. Our government did not expect or plan the assassinations, but it did nothing to prevent them. No one who knew the situation there could have believed that there would be a bloodless coup d'etat.

Another Ngo brother, Ngo Dinh Can, was executed soon afterwards. He had gone to the U.S. Consulate in Hue, where he was promised safe conduct to American protection in Saigon. Upon landing at Ton Son Nhut airport in a U.S. aircraft, he was turned over to the new government of South Vietnam, put before a firing squad, and shot. He was a diabetic, scarcely able to stand. I am told that he scornfully rejected the eyeband offered him.

Three weeks later, John Kennedy was dead, murdered in Dallas. As Eisenhower had passed serious problems in Vietnam on to him, so Kennedy left Lyndon Johnson the consequences of his actions. The overthrow of the constitutional government in Vietnam created a political vacuum there. Throughout the country the situation deteriorated rapidly. The Viet Cong and Hanoi immediately seized their opportunity. The strategic hamlets were attacked and began to be wiped out. The civil government officials, including the province chiefs, did not know what to do, with everybody getting crossed signals from the military junta. Although many Saigon residents rejoiced in the streets after the coup, most Vietnamese in the countryside were shocked and disillusioned. The Viet Cong were delighted. "We could not believe," said a Viet Cong leader, "the Americans would be so stupid as to undermine Diem."

From what I saw during his visit in May 1961 and in the meetings we both attended in August and early September 1963, I thought that Vice President Johnson's judgment on Vietnam was sound. Like all of us, he had not been satisfied with the pace of progress there, but had judged that it was better to keep on the course our government had first selected than to change direction. His assumption of the Presidency gave Johnson the opportunity to repair some of the damage in Vietnam. He had the chance to say, "We made a mistake. Now we are going to take a new look at our commitment in Vietnam."

With this in mind, I sent a hand-written note to the new President, saying, in effect: "Mr. President, you have inherited a situation which I regard as a political vacuum in Vietnam. I do not predict any good things from the military junta as political leaders. If that judgment is correct, I would hope you would not get too close to any of the military leaders." I then watched with growing misgivings as President Johnson publicly hailed Big Minh, and later as Secretary McNamara, acting for the administration, embraced General Nguyen Khanh, who overthrew Minh in the first of a series of generals' coups. There were nine governments in Saigon in a span of two years.

On February 25, 1964, I sent President Johnson another letter:

Dear Mr. President:

I am sorry to have been unable to get an appointment to see you, for I have wanted for several months to talk with you about Vietnam and related matters. I believe you and I have seen the issues in Vietnam in much the same light from the time of your visit there in May, 1961; at least, I have that impression from talks we have had in the past. I know, therefore, how heavily this problem must now weigh on your mind, as indeed it does on mine also, and I earnestly hope that, despite certain irrevocable errors that I think have been made, a way can yet be found to fulfill our national interests there with honor.

I take the liberty of sending this letter, Mr. President, because I feel an obligation as well as a desire to tell you frankly and directly about my future course of action, which is likely to be interpreted in the press and elsewhere as being related to my tour of duty in Vietnam.

I have today sent to the Secretary of State a request to be granted retirement from the Foreign Service, in order to accept an offer in private business. That my decision has been influenced by my strong disapproval of certain actions which were taken last fall in relation to Vietnam, with predictable adverse consequences, I do not deny. Nor do I deny that I have been uncomfortable in my association with the Department of State since returning from Vietnam six month ago.

Under these circumstances, it seems sensible for me to accept a position in private business. As a private citizen, I shall continue to do my best to contribute to our country's success.

I solicit your understanding, Mr. President, and I wish for you, as you know, personal happiness and all success in looking after the affairs of our nation.

Sincerely and respectfully yours,

Frederick E. Nolting

I saw President Johnson once or twice after my retirement from the Foreign Service. I recall particularly a comment he made to me the following summer. My wife and I were attending a White House ceremony honoring Paul Harkins upon his return from Vietnam in 1964. During a brief conversation after the ceremony, the President referred to my earlier note, in which I had urged him to distance himself from the military junta and encourage a return to a civilian government. "I had your letter," he told me, "and I agree with you. But I cannot now repudiate my predecessor's commitments." I interpreted that to mean that after the November elections, changes might be made.

But the chain of miscalculations was inexorable. The South Vietnamese military heads of government, one after another, proved incapable of governing. The Viet Cong and Hanoi stepped up the pressure, and the South began to crumble. By early 1965, President Johnson and his inherited cabinet advisors, principally Rusk and McNamara, themselves committed to the new Vietnamese leaders, were faced with a stark choice—either to accept the fall of Saigon or to send in American combat forces. They chose the latter course.

Cabot Lodge was reappointed by Johnson as Ambassador to South Vietnam in 1965. I have never understood why. I know that Vice President Johnson disapproved of much of Lodge's advice and many of his actions under Kennedy in 1963. Why, then, did he reappoint him? I can only speculate, but I suspect that Johnson, like Kennedy, wanted a thick piece of Republican asbestos out there to shield him from the heat. He might also have calculated that the man who had encouraged the generals to seize power would be able to curb their jealousies and guide their actions.

In any event, the intensity of the war increased. It became, in effect, a war between the United States and North Vietnam until our final withdrawal in 1974.

The two American presidents who bore the brunt of the "American War" in Vietnam, Lyndon Johnson and Richard Nixon, had much to say about the overthrow of the Diem government.

In his memoires, *The Vantage Point*, President Johnson gave his early reactions:

I told Lodge and the others that I had serious misgivings. Many people were criticizing the removal of Diem and were shocked by his murder. Congressional demands for our withdrawal from Vietnam were becoming louder and more insistent. I thought we had been mistaken in our failure to support Diem. But all that, I said, was behind us. Now we had to concentrate on accomplishing our goals. We had to help the new government get on its feet and perform effectively.... I had one important reservation about this generally hopeful assessment. I believed the assassination of President Diem had created more problems for the Vietnamese than it had solved. I saw little evidence that men of experience and ability were available in Vietnam, ready to help lead their country. I was deeply concerned that worse political turmoil might lie ahead in Saigon.... There were profound regrets in Washington, as there should have been. Those regrets deepened as political confusion swept in waves over Saigon in the following months. But then it was too late to reconsider.[13]

At a press conference in 1971, President Richard Nixon was quite candid: "I would remind all concerned that the way we got into Vietnam was through overthrowing Diem and the complicity in the murder of Diem."[14]

Before he died in 1985, Ambassador Cabot Lodge sent a letter to his old friend, Corliss Lamont, with whom he had long disagreed on Vietnam policy. It was published in the *Harvard Magazine* in November 1985.

Dear Corliss,

Regarding your open letter of November 1, 1965, concerning me—you were right—We were wrong and we failed—I should have resigned sooner.

Thank you for your most interesting book which I am reading with avidity.

Best wishes always,

Cabot

August 2, 1984.

One can only wish that others involved in this tragic era would be so frank.

Conclusion

After the overthrow of the constitutional government of South Vietnam in November 1963, I felt that our cause in Vietnam was lost. I could see no possible recovery from that mistake, but I hoped for many years that my judgment would prove to be wrong. Indeed, if the Johnson administration (and the Congress and people of this country) had opted for an unlimited war, the conclusion would undoubtedly have been different but the ultimate consequences dangerously unpredictable.

To most Americans the most vivid and poignant years are the eight years (1965–1973) when more than 2 million of our citizens fought in the Vietnam War. Fifty-eight thousand Americans lost their lives there, and uncounted more were permanently injured or afflicted in body or mind. This account does not go into those years, about which so much has been written. But I do want to stress one point: our failure in Vietnam was the result of political, not military, mistakes. As a part of the diplomatic branch of our government, my admiration and respect for the members of our armed forces who served in Vietnam, during and after my time, is deep and sincere. From the early military advisors (volunteers all) to the last of the 2.5 million draftees to leave Vietnam, they did their duty under strict civilian direction and control. When I outline, as I see them, the causes of an unnecessary war, I trust that I will not be misunderstood, especially by those who suffered most from the blunders of our political leaders.

The link between the overthrow of the Diem government of South Vietnam in 1963 and the "American" war that followed is now, I think, clear to most people. What obscured that linkage for many years was the tragic assassination of President Kennedy, which cast a pall of shock and sorrow over America and blurred our vision and judgment. The change in the nature of the struggle in South Vietnam from 1964 onward involved two main elements: the incompetence of the South Vietnamese military junta and its successive leaders, and Hanoi's decision to exploit to the fullest the political vacuum in the South. To these must be added a moral or psychological factor, namely, the

U.S. government's feeling that we were somehow obligated to support the factions we had helped to install in power. If we did not do so, it was argued, we would not only lose Southeast Asia to communism. We would also—and this was the unspoken consideration—have to reveal the fact that the Kennedy administration had blundered. President Johnson inherited a rapidly deteriorating situation in South Vietnam, which drove him (mistakenly, in my view) into taking over Vietnam's struggle and trying to win it through military means.

Was it an impossible task in the early 1960s to defeat the Viet Cong insurgency and also bring less authoritarian rule to Vietnam? Reconciling these two conflicting interests was our government's basic problem under Kennedy. I do not think that it was impossible, although it was surely difficult. One of our most serious mistakes was the failure to assign clear priorities to U.S. interests. Were the subjugation of the Viet Cong insurgency and pacification of the country prerequisites to the liberalization of the Diem regime? In retrospect, I think they were, but this never became clear in our instructions or in our actions. There were, of course, differences of opinion on this issue. In general, I think it is fair to say that our mission in Saigon was more realistic on the question than were our superiors in Washington, particularly those in the State Department and the White House. In Saigon we felt that liberalization of the GVN could be expected, but only after a measure of peace and stability was achieved. From this it followed that we in Saigon tended to stress the need for more efficiency in the GVN. Sometimes this involved more liberalism and democracy—but sometimes it did not, depending on the areas, the people, the available local leaders, and the issues. Further from the scene and its daily frustrations and encouragements, Washington's views were different. They were more politically motivated and less practical. "Authoritarianism" is a dirty word in the United States—much more so than in Southeast Asia—but it is a relative term. Where lives and property were at stake, protection, stability, and justice were uppermost in the minds of most Vietnamese.

President Diem and his brother Ngo Dinh Nhu were not power-hungry men, but certainly they looked upon the Viet Cong insurgency as their number one concern. If the United States had been equally clear in its priorities in the early 1960s, much trouble would have been avoided. A more representative, less authoritarian government would probably have developed under President Diem behind an effective shield of protection and security, together with economic and social benefits for the Vietnamese people. It was in fact evolving in the early sixties: as examples, while I was there, the Village Election Law was put into effect in many areas to elect village elders, or mayors; a National Economic Advisory Council was established; and, of course, elections for the members of the National Assembly were held regularly. However, an

American-style democracy would have taken many years to come about—if, indeed, it would ever have suited the Vietnamese people.

Some writers explain our deepening involvement as the inevitable consequence of our country's decision to help South Vietnam after the treaty that divided Vietnam in 1954. I hold a different opinion. I think the United States was right in its decisions, under Eisenhower and Kennedy, to help South Vietnam, on both moral and strategic grounds. Our early commitments were limited ones; the consequences were not inevitable. America's mistakes leading to war were political, not military. I shared in those mistakes, and I suffer the same haunting nightmares as many veterans do.

The agreements with the Diem government by both Eisenhower and Kennedy were based explicitly on the premise that South Vietnam was responsible for its own defense. Our government agreed to help, not to shoulder the responsibility. President Kennedy went further than President Eisenhower had gone in promising U.S. help to South Vietnam, both in military assistance, material, and training and in moral support. The joint U.S.-GVN communiqué at the time of Vice President Johnson's visit to Saigon in May 1961 clearly reveals this. But there was no commitment to use American forces to defend South Vietnam.

Most important, there was an explicit understanding between Kennedy and Diem that the United States would not interfere in the internal affairs of South Vietnam. Diem insisted upon this, and Kennedy readily agreed. "Interference in internal affairs" is not a precise phrase. But can anyone deny that American actions vis-à-vis the Diem government in the latter part of 1963 violated the very core of noninterference? Was our demand that President Diem dismiss Counselor Nhu in violation of our pledge of noninterference in internal affairs? Was our plotting with the dissident Vietnamese generals to overthrow their elected constitutional government a violation of our pledge of noninterference? There can be no question but that they were.

These breaches of promise constituted the moral link leading to American participation in the war. A week after his arrival in Saigon, Ambassador Lodge invoked a false moral argument when he cabled Washington: "We are launched on a course from which there is no responsible turning back: the overthrow of the Diem Government." U.S. collusion in the coup against Diem was the antithesis of moral responsibility.

America's actions in the fall of 1963 were spurred by the Kennedy administration's fears that our long effort to sustain South Vietnam would be wiped out by the failure of the Diem government to cope successfully with the Buddhist crisis. This fear was, I believe, based on a false assessment of the actual situation in Vietnam, but that is not the point I wish to emphasize here. The fundamental point is that, whatever Washington's reading of the situation was, our government had no justification whatsoever for breaking America's pledge to its ally. That pledge was made in the name of the American people. It was a pledge that we would not use our power, or our influence, to interfere in the internal politics of South Vietnam. Our government went back on that pledge in 1963. Some say that no other alternatives were open to us. That is not correct. It was clearly possible at that time either to continue our support of South Vietnam through its legitimate constitutional government or to withdraw. Instead, we encouraged dissident generals to revolt. When on November 1, 1963, the coup occurred, our top officials said that America had nothing to do with it. That, to my mind, was inexcusable. It was the cause of my decision to resign from the government.

The impact of the war in Vietnam proved greater and more enduring than many people realize; greater in terms of American opinion and policy, and greater in terms of maintaining a reasonable balance of power on our small, divided planet.

The reaction I feared most from our losses and failure was a permanent swing in American opinion toward isolation. Forunately, this did not occur. We might have sustained much more damage as a world power than we did from our loss in Vietnam. The residual lesson seems to be a more realistic view of our power and influence—more humility perhaps, more caution, but certainly not a retreat from world affairs. Where our vital interests are involved—and that is always the most difficult judgment—our national stance seems again vigilant and strong.

Over the years, many questions have been raised concerning the lessons to be learned from our experience in Vietnam. How should we apply them to other situations around the world, from Iran to Angola, El Salvador, Nicaragua, the Philippines, and many other problems present and future? I have never been able to discover any exact parallels. Each situation involving intervention or nonintervention is different, and where intervention appears to be in our nation's vital interest, the means and capabilities at our disposal must be carefully considered. To many of my former students at the University of Virginia, this kind of response seemed like a cop-out. But I think one can only draw general, not specific, lessons from Vietnam. Most of these are self-evident. Many fall into the category of moral, rather than practical, considerations.

In the first place, I think we Americans tend to underestimate the rationality and judgment of other persons, countries, and peoples in matters concerning their own destiny and well being. My instincts are noninterventionist in other countries' internal politics. This may seem simplistic in our present world, with all its rivalries, pressures, and skullduggery. Nevertheless, in both moral and practical terms, I think American physical intervention, whether covert or overt, has generally been unproductive. Again, except where our vital national interests are involved (World War II is a prime example), I believe American interventionist tendencies should be curbed.

In their place, I think far greater reliance should be placed on diplomacy. NATO, for example, is certainly a military alliance, but its principal achievements have come through patient, long-range diplomacy between its members and vis-à-vis the Soviet Union and its allies. In the case of Vietnam, our country ran out of patience and diplomacy in 1963—to our ultimate sorrow and defeat. It is ironic that our State Department was the principal advocate of revolution there, whereas our military establishment and the CIA were strongly opposed. To be successful, diplomacy must be consistent, long-range, patient, and firm. Our appointed ambassadors should be trusted, corrected when necessary, or removed. They should never be left in the dark. Above all, they should never be given false information to be conveyed to governments to which they are accredited.

Straightforward, consistent diplomatic persuasion can and should play a fundamental role in our dealings with other nations—much more than it has in the recent past. This is particularly true when we are dealing with countries whose histories, backgrounds, customs, and beliefs are basically different from our own. Misunderstandings based on differing national temperaments and attitudes are at the root of many of our international problems. Wise diplomacy, rather than threats or shows of force, can resolve many issues, and in the process we ourselves can learn to be more patient, more understanding, and more tolerant of others.

Finally, I think that our policies toward other nations must be deeply rooted in principles which the American people will support in the long run. I have faith enough to believe that these include honesty, fairness, compassion, a sense of justice, and a capacity to understand the underlying facts if clearly presented. In short, America's integrity—not the image, but the reality—is the most important asset we have.

POSTSCRIPT

In 1975, former Secretary of State Dean Rusk published a letter in the *Norfolk Ledger-Star* concerning my recall from Vietnam. He was provoked into doing so by a letter in the same paper saying that I had been "jerked" from my post and that this had brought on disastrous consequences. His reply said that I had resigned at my own request, against his personal efforts to persuade me to stay on the job. With reluctance, I sent the letter which follows and include it here for the record.

April 25, 1975

The Honorable Dean Rusk
University of Georgia
School of Law
Athens, Georgia 30602

Dear Dean,

I have read your note of April 16 to Col. Addison Hagan which he sent me, and your letter to the Norfolk Ledger-Star, published April 22. Recriminations regarding Vietnam are petty and unproductive, as I'm sure you will agree, but the factual record is something else. Your statements concerning my recall from Saigon are simply not true in the context in which you place them, nor in their implication. I regret to have to state this so bluntly after our long association, but there is a matter of personal integrity involved. I intend to publish this letter in reply to your published letter.

You may recall our exchange in 1964, after my resignation from government service following my unsuccessful attempts to prevent the undermining of the Diem government. Several members of the House Foreign Affairs Committee told me that you had testified that I resigned as ambassador "when the going got rough." I challenged your statement then and received from you a brief denial. Now you raise the same matter publicly and imply that I quit my job under fire. I am compelled to recite the facts, some of which you may have forgotten.

In April 1961 before our departure to Vietnam, you and I had a talk in your office. During that talk, I raised the question of how long my tour of duty would be. You agreed that two years would be about right, adding that "the way things are going out there, we will be lucky to have a mission there for six months."

Over the next two years, the situation in South Vietnam improved markedly. As Secretary of State, you yourself frequently testified to that effect. Towards the end of the two year period, during a relatively calm time, I wrote you from Saigon reminding you of our understanding and suggesting that a successor be sought and an orderly transfer arranged in due course. After a prolonged delay, I received a message from Averell Harriman, instructing me to stay on indefinitely. I responded to that by referring to our earlier understanding and the reasons for it, and again urged that a suitable replacement be found and an orderly transfer made. Subsequently, I received a message saying that our government was looking for a replacement. The Department suggested that my family and I should come to Washington on home leave, taking a vacation enroute, and return to Saigon for an indefinite period until a successor was appointed. We left Saigon on May 23 on State Department travel orders, which read "To Washington via Europe and return."

The timing of our six weeks leave could not have been worse. The Buddhist crisis broke during my absence. I was not informed of this either by the State Department or by our Embassy in Saigon (who had our daily schedule and address with the understanding that I would be notified of any change in the situation). I received no word from either source until our arrival in New York on July 1. While crossing the Atlantic, I heard of Ambassador Lodge's appointment by ship's radio. After a brief trip to Washington, I returned immediately to Saigon. Seeing the gravity of the situation there, I urgently requested permission from Washington to stay on as long as necessary to help calm the agitation and restore confidence. This request was answered by instructions to leave Vietnam by August 15, before Ambassador Lodge's arrival.

I will always be deeply distressed by the fact that I was absent from my post at a time of major crisis. However, I cannot and do not accept your statement: "I personally made an effort to persuade Nolting to stay on his job in a conversation in my office in Washington." This is not true. I have no recollection of any such conversation at or near the time of my recall. My request to be replaced was made much earlier, under totally different circumstances, and was related to an orderly transfer of responsibility in a period of relative calm and progress. My later request from Saigon to stay on the job during the Buddhist crisis was denied by a telegram signed "Rusk."

To what extent you were personally involved in, or aware of, the chain of events leading to my recall I do not know. You had a great deal on your mind and it never seemed to me that Vietnam, at that time, was one of your major preoccupations—as it later became. You spoke of a "Diem must go" group in Washington, describing them as "some younger people." It may well be that some of the messages you sent me never arrived and that some I sent you never came to your attention.

I should add that *had* I been instructed to act as my successor did—namely, to encourage a coup détat—I would have refused to do so, and resigned. My position on that was well known in Washington, in particular to Averell Harriman.

Other points you made in your letter to the Ledger-Star require comment.

You said: "It was not the policy of the Kennedy administration to overthrow President Diem." The Pentagon Papers, to the contrary, state that you as Secretary of State cabled the Embassy in Saigon: "The U.S. Government will support a coup which has a good chance of succeeding but plans no direct involvement of U.S. armed forces." Ambassador Lodge is reported to have cabled the State Department: "We are launched on a course from which there is no respectable turning back: the overthrow of the Diem Government." If Ambassador Lodge was not speaking for the Kennedy Administration, why was he not restrained or recalled by the President?

Summing up the Kennedy Administration's role, the Pentagon Papers state: "For the military coup détat against Ngo Dinh Diem, the U.S. must accept its full share of responsibility." That is the verdict of a non-partisan U.S. Government fact-finding group with access to official classified documents. My own participation in the debates in Washington and my personal observation of U.S. Government actions at the time strongly confirm that conclusion. I find it hard to believe that you could make the statements you did in your published letter. I must conclude that with all your responsibilities at the time, you relegated this problem to subordinates who deceived you.

Sincerely yours,

[signed]
Frederick E. Nolting, Jr.

In a personal reply, my old friend stuck to his accusation, saying that he would try to have someone check his records in Washington for the date of the alleged conversation in his office. After thirteen years, no confirmation or denial has been received. It is a minor matter, but somehow to me it

typifies the Kennedy administration's handling of the Vietnam crisis of 1963—
a record of confusion, duplicity, and fatal errors. I say this with regret and
sadness, mindful of the achievements of the Kennedy administration at other
times and in other areas.

Notes

1. Bao Dai was the former emperor of Central Vietnam, installed by the French as ruler of Indo-China in 1949.

2. The Vietminh (Vietnamese nationalists) were the supporters of Ho Chi Minh, the Communist organizer and leader of the movement for independence of Vietnam since the early 1930s. They were the core of the opposition to French rule and to Japanese occupation of Vietnam during World War II. Many other Vietnamese nationalists (non-Communists) fought alongside the French from 1945 to 1954.

3. For the text of the communiqué, see U.S. Department of State *Bulletin*, June 19, 1961, pp. 956–957.

4. Following is a telegram I sent to the Department of State that illustrates such comments:

Telegram From the Embassy in Vietnam to the Department of State

Saigon, July 14, 1961—7p.m.

70. Deptel 35 to Saigon. Have for weeks been seeking answers to questions like those posed reference telegram. My reading of situation and prospects here, tending towards optimism, is neither static nor final, and is of course fallible. Views of high-caliber country team here difficult to pin down in common denominator, since assessments vary. Diplomats of friendly countries Saigon also not unanimous in their views, generally inclined to be more pessimistic than US. Intelligent and patriotic Vietnamese citizens, and even GVN officials, not of one accord re prospects of country or re necessary measures.

The following then are my personal views. I shall invite other members task force to forward their comments, if they see matters differently in general or in any particulars.

In the two months that I have been here I have traveled widely in country, generally in company President Diem and several of his cabinet. Have also spent many hours in private conversation with Diem, whom I like and admire as a person. The trips have been worthwhile, I think, despite fact that much of what I saw was dressed up for President's visit. (I feel certain that [Diem] would prefer to see things in the raw, and was not trying particularly to impress me; but a certain amount of artificiality is nevertheless built into such visits.) Trips have extended to all areas of Vietnam, including about 100 kilometers of Laotian border, except far north, which I hope to visit soon. They have provided opportunity to compare conditions and attitudes other sections of country with those in Saigon.

Distinction should be made, I think, between two aspects of situation here, often confused: (A) What is Vietnamese Government (which means President Diem) striving for? Are his philosophy, objectives, and moral values sound in terms US interests in world? (B) How are these being put into effect? How are they being understood and received by Vietnamese people? Is progress rapid enough to keep pace with increased pressure? If not, what can be done about it?

Regarding (A), I think President Diem's philosophy of government, and his objectives for his country, are sound and good. After many hours of fundamental discussions, I am convinced that he is no dictator, in the sense of relishing power for its own sake. On the contrary, he seems to me to be a man dedicated to high principles by himself and his people; a man who would prefer to be a monk rather than a political leader; a man who does not fundamentally enjoy power or the exercise of it. He is, nevertheless, an egoist in the sense that he believes (in my judgment, with some justification) that he can govern in South Vietnam, in general and in detail, better than anyone else now available; and that he knows more about the Communist movement in this area and how to combat it than anyone else. His own strong convictions, energy, and his faith in himself are both a strength and a weakness—a strength in providing a counter-dynamic to communism, a weakness in causing overconcentration of governmental power and authority, consequent lack of governmental efficiency, and in offering a vulnerable political target. His philosophy of government, summed up in the term "personalism" (which does not mean personal dictatorship but rather the requirement for individual development much in the Aristotelian sense) is perhaps too lofty for popular understanding, but is certainly in my judgment sound and right, and compatible with US interests. (Please note July 7 expression of this philosophy sent Task Force Washington.) Thus, I think the United States should have no hesitation on moral grounds in backing Diem to the hilt. Where we think he is wrong, we can bring about ameliorations and improvements gradually in proportion to the confidence which he has in us and in his ability to make concessions without slipping.

Re (B), my (Limit Distribution) assessment is less clear-cut. There is no question that Diem and his government have felt an increasing upsurge of confidence in the US over the past 6 months, despite developments in Laos. High US expressions of support, backed by concrete and continuing actions, have had real effect. First commandment of task force report—to build confidence—was, in my judgment, soundly conceived, is being carried out, and is being reciprocated. Strong and evident US support has brought to the government side a certain number of fence sitters, and has also probably considerably reduced the likelihood of a military coup d'etat. It has at the same time made Diem an even more vulnerable target of Communist attack, which has, I fear, carried some people into the enemy's camp. Diem himself realizes this and that is why he is so eager to get across the thought that victory of the Vietnamese people over Communist subversion has [to be] gained through Vietnamese sacrifice and not directly through American or free world protection. Nevertheless, I do not think it is true that US support has given President Diem's government as yet a net increase in popularity among the Vietnamese people. Oddly enough, Diem's own keen personal interest in and knowledge of [practical] things of life, such as farming, fishing, disease, teaching methods, construction methods and techniques, are misinterpreted or distorted by many Vietnamese into the picture of a remote and aloof man who has little interest in the welfare of the common man. This is due in part, I think, to his manner and in part to Communist propaganda. It is definitely a false picture, judging from many trips and much discussion. In any case, it seems to me clear that in some way the Diem government must make a "break-through" to regain popular support. If the situation drags on in an inconclusive manner for many more months, either a military coup, or an open proclamation of a Communist Government and widespread civil war, is likely.

I agree that the key to such a break-through is sufficient military and security forces, and skillful selection thereof, to guarantee protection and a free choice to the people in Vietnam, especially in the country districts. At present, despite all efforts, this protection does not exist in many areas. In fact, while accurate statistics on the degree of security are not obtainable, and while the situation varies from province-to-province and from district-to-district, I do not believe that the net security situation is any better now than it was 2 months ago. There have been some encouraging statistics, such as the percentage of actions being initiated by government forces against Viet Cong forces against 75 percent initiated by VC four months ago, which in turn seems to reflect more intelligence coming in from countryside. (This ratio has recently slipped again.) On the other hand, there are reports of very large losses of rice to Viet Cong (being checked and reported separately), instances of refusal from fear to identify assassins, and the establishment of VC "governments" parallel to GVN authority in some areas, collecting taxes and issuing VC money. All of which adds up to a very [mixed] picture, but one which is certainly not conclusively getting better. In our attempt to help create a new and winning psychology, I have taken a much more optimistic line in conversations with other diplomats and with press here than that reflected above, and I think we should continue to do so, giving benefit of the doubt wherever possible to optimistic assessment.

Re security situation in Saigon itself, there is no evident change over past several months, aside from shooting up of USOM officer Davis's car about ten miles out of Saigon a week ago, and grenade attempt at me last Saturday. We have been trying to figure out what these mean in terms of security of Americans here, but cannot be categoric. Facts are that no arrests made to date in either incident. There was reluctance on the part of eye witnesses to Davis' shooting to testify or identify assailant. Vietnamese police and sûreté are conscientiously working on cases, but no concrete results to date. After a study, we have gotten out a note to Americans here, based on conclusion that recent attacks do not seem to foreshadow wider terrorist activities against Americans, but recommending increased prudence and circumspection.

MAAG is writing detailed evaluation of recent sweep in Vinh Binh Province, which should be ready shortly. My impressions to date are that combined operation, first of its kind, was fairly efficient and effective militarily, the most of Viet-Cong escaped net, and that while much territory was liberated, there is question as to who will control it after bulk of forces withdrawn. Some Ranger battalions are being left there, and some civic action being undertaken by army units. In general, however, it appears that this sweep points up the long-felt need of utmost coordination between military actions and quick follow-up on social and economic programs. We have not licked this problem yet.

Re GVN reforms in military command, intelligence, economic and social fields, the following is a quick personal assessment.

Military command: Despite some reports to contrary, my evaluation is that reform in military command is producing many desired results, and will produce more. Diem's proclivity to interfere with military authority will be further reduced as his own confidence in US support and in loyalty his military forces increases. Confidence on both fronts is increasing.

Intelligence: While GVN central intelligence organization not yet fully functioning, prospects are good and we expect increasing results.

Economic and social measures: Work of Staley group with Vietnamese opposite numbers, resulting in effective briefing of Diem and Cabinet July 11th, has opened new prospect and given real boost to possibilities in these fields. This, added to continued effective work of USOM and USIS, plus greater emphasis on part GVN as reflected in recent Cabinet shifts, hold prospects of increasing success. Much depends on US backing and particularly on greater flexibility and promptness to follow-through.

Re effective central planning, we have come up with a recommendation, embodied in joint briefing July 11 and accepted by Diem, of a mechanism which promises to produce more effective planning and implementation of joint programs. We must assure that these programs bear the stamp "Made in Viet-Nam" rather than "Made in America", and we must keep constantly on alert lest oral or written undertakings by GVN substitute for concrete end products—something which can happen here.

In general, I am optimistic. I believe we [are] taking the right track. It is a question of how fast and effectively we can advance.

Nolting

(Source: Department of State, Central Files, 751K.00/7–1461. Secret; Priority; Limit Distribution. Repeated to CINCPAC for PolAd, Vientiane, Bangkok, London, Geneva for FECON, Phnom Penh, and Paris.)

5. The International Control Commission issued a public report to the UN in 1961 in which it condemned both North Vietnam and South Vietnam for violations of the Geneva Accords. However, the report came down much harder on the Hanoi gov-

ernment than on the Saigon government, saying, in effect, that South Vietnam was acting in self-defense against the insurgency in the South that was inspired and supported by Hanoi. The Commission's vote on the report was split, with India and Canada voting in support of it, and with Poland voting against it.

6. The purpose of the agrovilles and of the strategic hamlets was the same, to offer greater protection to the peasant farmers and their families against Viet Cong raids and their demands for food and recruits. The difference was in the size, location, and approach to resettlement. The Strategic Hamlets program was based on voluntary regrouping, self-defense, and less government involvement. In consequence, it was more popular with the peasants.

7. I spoke in English; translations were distributed in Vietnamese and French.

8. David Halberstam, "The Americanization of Vietnam," 1969.

9. Some months after the *coup*, I was talking with a journalist friend in Washington about our ineffectiveness in Saigon with most of the press and media. He said: "You need not blame yourself too much. During the months in which you were receiving those urgent instructions from Washington to change the press' attitude, Averell Harriman was having private chats with newsmen and editors here, saying 'Diem must go.' I was one of them."

10. On the invitation of President Diem, the General Assembly of the United Nations sent a delegation to Vietnam to investigate and report on alleged violations of human rights by the Government of South Vietnam, in particular the allegations raised in the U.N. of religious persecution. The mission arrived in Saigon on October 24, 1963, at the height of the Buddhist crisis and the coup plotting. Its chairman was Ambassador Abdul Rahman Paghwak of Afghanistan. Other members represented Brazil, Costa Rica, Ceylon, Dahomey, Morocco, and Nepal.

The U.N. mission was given full access to all persons it wished to interview, in private and with no government representatives present. It talked with many people, Buddhist, Christian, and others. The mission came up with no definite conclusions. The coup d'état interrupted its investigations on November 1–2, and the delegation left Vietnam on November 3, 1963.

The United Nations dropped the matter. The chairman of the commission said later that no definite evidence of religious persecution or violations of human rights by the Government of South Vietnam had been found. See U.N. General Assembly, 18th Session Agenda, Item 77, December 7, 1963.

11. Bill Trueheart and I had known each other for many years. I had requested his assignment to Saigon two years earlier. I admired his hard work and efficiency and relied heavily upon him. So, in the final analysis, I have only myself to blame for my misplaced confidence in him.

12. George C. Herring, *America's Longest War: The U.S. and Vietnam, 1950–1975* (New York: John Wiley & Sons, 1979), 100.

13. Lyndon Baines Johnson, *Vantage Point: Perspectives of the Presidency, 1963–1969* (New York: Holt, Rinehart, and Winston, 1971), 43–46, 62.

14. "Public Papers of the Presidents of the United States: Richard M. Nixon." Official transcript. *Foreign Relations of the United States, 1961–1963*, vol. 1, Vietnam 1961, page 292.

Selected Bibliography

BOOKS AND PERIODICALS

Ball, George. *The Past Has Another Pattern: Memoirs*. New York: W. W. Norton & Co., 1982.

Bohlen, Charles E. *Witness to History, 1929–1969*. New York: W. W. Norton & Co., 1973

Bowles, Chester. *Promises to Keep: My Years in Public Life, 1941–1969*. New York: Harper & Row, 1971.

Buttinger, Joseph. *Vietnam: A Dragon Embattled*, 2 vols. Vol. II, *Vietnam at War*. New York: Praeger, 1967.

Cao Van Luan. *Ben Giong Lich Su: Hoi Ky 1940–65*. Saigon: Tri Dung, 1972.

Carver, George A. "The Real Revolution in South Viet Nam." *Foreign Affairs* (April 1969).

Chaffard, Georges. *Les Deux guerres du Vietnam*. Paris: La Table Ronde, 1969.

Charlton, Michael, and Anthony Moncrieff. *Many Reasons Why: The American Involvement in Vietnam*. New York: Hill and Wang, 1978.

Chen, King C. "Haoni's Three Decisions and the Escalation of the Vietnam War." *Political Science Quarterly* 90 (Summer 1975): 239–259.

Colby, William. *Honorable Men: My Life in the CIA*. New York: Simon and Schuster, 1978.

Collins, James Lawton, Jr. *The Development and Training of the South Vietnamese Army, 1950–1972*. Washington: United States Government Printing Office, 1975.

Cooper, Chester L. *The Lost Crusade*. New York: Dodd, Mead & Co., 1970.

Duncanson, Dennis J. *Government and Revolution in Vietnam*. London: Oxford University Press, 1968.

Fall, Bernard B. *The Two Vietnams*. New York: Praeger, 1963.

FitzGerald, Frances. *Fire in the Lake: The Vietnamese and the Americans in Vietnam*. 1st ed. Boston: Little, Brown, 1972.

Futrell, Robert F. *The United States Air Force in Southeast Asia: The Advisory Years to 1965*. Washington: United States Government Printing Office, 1981.

Galbraith, John Kenneth. *Ambassador's Journal: A Personal Account of the Kennedy Years*. Boston: Houghton Mifflin, 1969.

———. *A Life in Our Times: Memoirs*. Boston: Houghton Mifflin, 1981.

Gelb, Leslie H. *The Irony of Vietnam: The System Worked*. Washington, D.C.: Brookings Institution, 1979.

Halberstam, David. *The Best and the Brightest*. New York: Random House, 1969.

————. *The Making of a Quagmire*. New York: Random House, 1965.

Hammer, Ellen. *A Death in November: America in Vietnam, 1963*. New York: E. P. Dutton, 1987.

Hannah, Norman B. *The Key to Failure: Laos and the Vietnam War*. New York: Madison Books, 1987.

Herring, George C. *America's Longest War: The United States and Vietnam, 1950–1975*. New York: John Wiley, 1979.

Higgins, Marguerite. *Our Vietnam Nightmare*. New York: Harper & Row, 1965.

Hilsman, Roger. *To Move a Nation*. Garden City, N.Y.: Doubleday, 1967.

Horowitz, David. *The Kennedys*. New York: Summit, 1984.

Humphrey, Hubert H. *The Education of a Public Man*. Garden City, N.Y.: Doubleday, 1976.

"Interview with Frederick E. Nolting, Jr., Former U.S. Ambassador to Saigon." *U.S. News & World Report*, July 26, 1971, pp. 67–70.

Johnson, Lyndon B. *The Vantage Point: Perspectives of the Presidency, 1963–1969*. New York: Holt, Rinehart and Winston, 1971.

Karnow, Stanley. *Vietnam: A History*. New York: Viking Press, 1983.

Kattenburg, Paul. *The Vietnam Trauma in American Foreign Policy, 1945–1975*. New Brunswick, N.J.: Transaction Books, 1980.

Lodge, Henry Cabot. *The Storm Has Many Eyes: A Personal Narrative*. New York: W. W. Norton & Co., 1973.

McCoy, Alfred, with Cathleen B. Read and Leonard P. Adams. *The Politics of Heroin in Southeast Asia*. New York: Harper & Row, 1972.

Maneli, Mieczyslaw. *War of the Vanquished*. New York: Harper & Row, 1971.

Mecklin, John. *Mission in Torment: An Intimate Account of the U.S. Role in Vietnam*. New York: Doubleday, 1965.

NBC News White Paper (transcript). "Death of Diem," December 22, 1971.

Nolting, Mrs. Frederick. "Clubwomen in Vietnam." *General Federation Clubwoman* (January 1965): 12–13, 30.

O'Ballance, Edgar. *The Wars in Vietnam, 1954–1980*. New York: Hippocrene Books, 1981.

Parmet, Herbert S. *JFK: The Presidency of John F. Kennedy*. New York: Dial Press, 1983.

Patti, Archimedes L. A. *Why Viet Nam?* Berkeley: University of California Press, 1980.

Powers, Thomas. *The Man Who Kept the Secrets*. New York: Alfred A. Knopf, 1979.

Rostow, Walt W. *The Diffusion of Power*. New York: Macmillan Co., 1972.

Rust, William J. *Kennedy in Vietnam*. New York: Scribner's, 1985.

Salinger, Pierre. *With Kennedy*. Garden City, N.Y.: Doubleday, 1966.

Santoli, Al. *To Bear Any Burden*. New York: E. P. Dutton, 1985.

Schlesinger, Arthur M., Jr. *Robert Kennedy and His Times*, 2 vols., vol. II. Boston: Houghton Mifflin, 1978.

————. *A Thousand Days: John F. Kennedy in the White House*. Boston: Houghton Mifflin, 1965.

Scigliano, Robert. *South Vietnam: Nation under Stress*. Boston: Houghton Mifflin, 1964.

Scigliano, Robert, and Guy Fox. *Technical Assistance in Vietnam: The Michigan State University Experience*. New York: Praeger, 1965.

Shaplen, Robert. *Time out of Hand: Revolution and Reaction in Southeast Asia*. New York: Harper & Row, 1969.

Sheehan, Neil. Letter to the Editor, *Washington Post*, June 24, 1974, p. A23.

Sorenson, Theodore C. *Kennedy*. New York: Bantam Books, 1966.

Spector, Ronald H. *United States Army in Vietnam, Advice and Support: The Early Years, 1941–1960*. Washington: Center of Military History, United States Government Printing Office, 1983.

Sullivan, Marianna P. *France's Vietnam Policy*. Westport, Conn.: Greenwood Press, 1978.

Taylor, Maxwell D. *Swords and Plowshares*. New York: W. W. Norton and Co., 1972.

Thompson, Robert. *Defeating Communist Insurgency*. London: Chatto & Windus, 1966.

Tran Van Don. *Our Endless War*. San Rafael, Calif.: Presidio Press, 1978.

Truong Nhu Tang. *A Vietcong Memoir*. New York: Harcourt Brace Jovanovich, 1985.

United States Department of State. *Bulletin*, January 1961–December 1963.

United States Senate. *Two Reports on Vietnam and Southeast Asia to the President of the United States by Senator Mike Mansfield*. Washington: United States Government Printing Office, 1973, pp. 7–14.

United States Senate. Committee on Foreign Relations. *The U.S. Government and the Vietnam War*, Part II, *1961–1964*, by the Congressional Research Service, Library of Congress, December 1984. Washington: United States Government Printing Office, 1985.

United States Senate. Select Committee to Study Governmental Operations. *Alleged Assassination Plots Involving Foreign Leaders*. Washington: United States Government Printing Office, 1975.

Vo Nguyen Giap. *Unforgettable Days*. Hanoi: Foreign Languages Publishing House, 1975.

Warner, Denis. *The Last Confucian: Vietnam, Southeast Asia, and the West*. Rev. ed. Sydney: Angus & Robertson, 1964.

Warner, Geoffrey. "The United States and the Fall of Diem, Part I." *Australian Outlook* (December 1974).

————. "The United States and the Fall of Diem, Part II." *Australian Outlook* (April 1975).

Whitlow, Robert H. *U.S. Marines in Vietnam: The Advisory and Combat Assistance Era, 1954–1964*. Washington: United States Government Printing Office, 1977.

DOCUMENTARY COLLECTIONS

The Declassified Documents Quarterly, 1975–1988. Washington: Carrollton Press, 1975–1981; Woodbridge, Conn: Research Publications, 1982–1988.

The Pentagon Papers: The Defense Department History of United States Decision-making on Vietnam [The Senator Gravel Edition]. Boston: Beacon Press, 1971.

Public Papers of the Presidents of the United States: John F. Kennedy, 1961. Washington: United States Government Printing Office, 1962.

Public Papers of the Presidents of the United States: John F. Kennedy, 1962. Washington: United States Government Printing Office, 1963.

Public Papers of the Presidents of the United States: John F. Kennedy, 1963. Washington: United States Government Printing Office, 1964.

Public Papers of the Presidents of the United States: Richard M. Nixon, 1971. Washington: United States Government Printing Office, 1972.

United States Department of Defense. *United States–Vietnam Relations, 1945–1967* [The Pentagon Papers]. Washington: United States Government Printing Office, 1971.

United States Department of State. *American Foreign Policy: Current Documents, 1961*. Washington: United States Government Printing Office, 1965.

———. *American Foreign Policy: Current Documents, 1962*. Washington: United States Government Printing Office, 1966.

———. *American Foreign Policy: Current Documents, 1963*. Washington: United States Government Printing Office, 1967.

———. *Foreign Relations of the United States, 1961–1963*, Vol. I, *Vietnam, 1961*. Washington: United States Government Printing Office, 1988. [Volumes covering 1962 and 1963 in process.]

United States Senate. Committee on Foreign Relations. *Executive Sessions of the Senate Foreign Relations Committee, Together with Joint Sessions with the Senate Armed Services Committee (Historical Series)*, Vol. XIV, *1962*. Washington: United States Government Printing Office, 1986.

PERSONAL COLLECTION OF FREDERICK E. NOLTING, JR.

Johnson, Lyndon B. Excerpt of an interview conducted by Ted Gittinger for the Oral History Program, Lyndon B. Johnson Library, Austin, Texas. Copy sent to the author by Ted Gittinger of the Johnson Library.

John F. Kennedy Library, Boston, Massachusetts. National Security Files, Vietnam Country Series. Assorted documents declassified under Mandatory Review.

Nolting, Frederick E. Interview conducted by Joseph E. O'Connor, May 14, 1966. Oral History Program, John F. Kennedy Library, Boston, Massachusetts.

———. Interview conducted by Dennis O'Brien, May 6, 1970. Oral History Program, John F. Kennedy Library, Boston, Massachusetts.

———. Interview conducted by Dennis O'Brien, May 7, 1970. Oral History Program, John F. Kennedy Library, Boston, Massachusetts.

———. Interview conducted by Anna Nelson and Patricia McAdams, December 7, 1978.

———. Interview conducted by Charles S. Sampson and Ronald D. Landa, April 25, 1984. Office of the Historian, United States Department of State.

———. Interview conducted by David M. Baehler and Louis J. Smith, June 1, 1984. Office of the Historian, United States Department of State.

———. "Kennedy Presidency and Foreign Policy," n.d. Transcript of presentation and question and answer session at the Miller Center, University of Virginia.

———. "The Origin and Development of United States Commitment in Vietnam." Address presented in Lynchburg, Virginia, April 2, 1968. Published as "The Turning Point," *Foreign Service Journal* (July 1968): 18–20.

———. Personal letter to Dean Rusk, April 25, 1975.

United Stated Department of State. Central Files. Assorted documents on Vietnam, 1961–1963, declassified under the Freedom of Information Act.

United States Embassy in Vietnam. Unclassified enclosures to unspecified document, 1963: Enclosure 1, "Outline: Vietnam—A Story of Nation Building While Fighting an Insurgency"; Enclosure 2, "Paper on Vietnam: A Story of Nation-Building While Fighting an Insurgency." Copies kept by the author upon final departure from Vietnam.

————. Unclassified airgram to the Department of State, number A–106, August 5, 1963, "Quarterly Economic Summary—April–June 1963." Copy kept by the author upon final departure from Vietnam.

Index

About the Author

FREDERICK NOLTING, Professor Emeritus at the University of Virginia, was the American Ambassador to South Vietnam from 1961 to 1963. Prior to that, he was assigned to NATO Headquarters and in 1957 became Deputy Chief of the U.S. Delegation to NATO and the Organization for European Economic Cooperation and Alternate U.S. Representative to the North Atlantic Council. Ambassador Nolting retired from the State Department in 1964 after twenty-two years of government service.

CPSIA information can be obtained at www.ICGtesting.com
Printed in the USA
LVOW13*0446060114

368191LV00003B/30/P